Adrenaline Addiction and the story of My Self-Destruction

Published by TTG Publishing

ISBN 978-0-578-27113-2

eISBN 979-8-88796-996-1

Library of Congress Cataloging-in-Publication Data

Printed in the United States of America

Adrenaline Addiction and the story of My Self -Destruction

I TELL YOU, MAN. I CAN MAKE IT!!
I THINK YOU'RE AN ADRENALINE JUNKIE, KARL.

Prologue

Addiction…when most people think of addiction, they think mostly of drugs, alcohol, gambling, smoking, etc. But what if there were another type of addiction that we as a society don't really think about? What if there were an addiction that can be just as destructive, but it's created naturally inside our bodies?

I'm talking about the one addiction that can be formed at any age and at any time in life, and that's adrenaline.

*When a person is face with a dangerous or frightening situation, the adrenal glands release adrenaline into the body. The body is prepared for the "fight or flight" response within minutes or even seconds. Adrenaline in the bloodstream causes several physical effects:

- Increased heart rate
- Heightened blood pressure
- Dilated pupils
- Quickened breathing

•

- Perspiration

As a result of adrenaline, a person may be faster, stronger, and more resistant to pain than normal. This is commonly known as the "adrenaline rush", a common effect that is a necessary survival mechanism. This powerful effect only lasts a short time before it wears off.

When looking at some obvious results of an adrenaline addiction, we can see there is an extreme danger to life and limb, especially when the behavior becomes more reckless with each passing day.

As with any type of addiction, the more you crave that addiction, the more risks you are willing to take. Eventually this leads those who are addicted to craving an even higher adrenaline rush and possibly more dangerous behaviors in order to reach that high.

*What's even more interesting are some of the signs that can be seen in someone who has an adrenaline addiction:

- Craving to participate in extreme or intense activities
- Losing interest in other hobbies or activities

- Suffering from withdrawal symptoms when they cannot participate in exciting activities
- A constant need to do even more exciting or dangerous activities
- Becoming more addicted to the effects of adrenaline with more experience
- Disregarding the potential risks of the activity

Throughout my life, I have experienced these symptoms along with others that have led to alcohol abuse to get an even higher adrenaline rush. Sometimes I would have to speed down the freeway at 100 m.p.h. drinking a bottle of rum, just to see how far I could push myself.
*Activities that can often produce adrenaline include:

- Driving unsafely
- Engaging in extreme sports like rock climbing, motorcycle racing, and skydiving
- Lying
- Gambling
- Stealing
- Abusing alcohol or drugs
- Picking a fight
- Having an argument

•

- Debating controversial issues
- Working after procrastination

I have also heard the term “adrenaline junkie” used but, I never truly grasped the meaning or even the consequences of what the addiction can lead to. I did, after all, see what the addiction can do to my mind set, causing me to make decisions that I would not rationally do.

With such a natural chemical made up inside our bodies, how can one be drawn to it in such a brief length of time?

In the end, adrenaline addiction can also lead you down a path of self-destruction in a matter of seconds.

This is the true story of a person who always wanted to feel the effects of getting an adrenaline high and, as a result, the self-destructive paths that resulted.

Some of the names have been altered in this story so as to not reveal their true identities

Chapter One

My very first taste of adrenaline goes back to when I was a student at a Montessori school. It was very strict and had very rigid guidelines; if you got out of line, you received one of many punishments.

The school gave off a creepy vibe, especially when I had seen the principal for the very first time. She was in a wheelchair and had the presence of, if you did the smallest thing wrong, she was going to make you feel like you were going to regret what you did for the rest of your life. Just the thought of being at that school made me feel all dirty and I wanted to escape the first chance I had.

Instead of playing with the other kids, I had taken to hiding out in a cabinet space for several hours. Like any kid at an early age, you try to learn from your teachers and other students to help make you grow, but for whatever reason, I could not go along with the program.

I was not fitting into their structure as I was reluctant to listen to what the teachers were telling me. All I wanted to do was hide out in my secret space until my dad came by to pick me up.

It was the crying from the other kids that got me the most. It seemed like, every hour one of the kids was being called up to the principals for the smallest infraction. The crying was constant and could be heard throughout the day.

The curriculum was awful; it seemed I was never learning anything because if you answered a question wrong, or even in the way the teacher was expecting you to answer, you were chastised in front of the entire class and made an example of it. That in itself made me not want to learn or for that matter, raise my hand to ask a question.

It didn't take me very long to decide I had enough of all the kids crying from the punishments and I didn't want to go back to that school anymore. I told myself I would do whatever it took not to go back into the classroom and avoid my turn in line for any punishment. In essence, that school was known for dishing out punishment with a yard stick.

When my dad pulled up to school to drop me off, I didn't budge an inch and just sat there in the car. Dad told me I needed to get to school before I was late, but still I sat in the seat not moving an inch. I refused to get out of the car because I wanted nothing to do with the school anymore.

He finally had enough so he got out of his seat and reached back to force me out of the car. I wasn't going to let that happen and decided I would jump around the seats to keep him from taking me out of the car. I would start from the back seat and every time he would open the door, I would continuously jump from the back to the front and vice versa.

It was getting a bit wild, and everyone was starting to watch, curious to see what was going on, staring at both of us. I had one hundred percent refused to get out and I put all of my might into staying in the car and not going into that dreaded class. So, I started yelling very loudly and I even kicked and punched my dad away so I did not have to go back to that school!

But he was determined one way or another to get me out of the car. I don't remember exactly how he did it, but after all the noise and turmoil I was making, he finally got me out of the car and sent me on my way to the classroom. It is an understatement to say I was not very happy about my circumstances and I was constantly thinking of how I was going to do the same thing the next day because this place was bad news!

When I got to class and the day finally got started, I calmed down and went about learning. After a few hours had passed, there was an incident in one of the classrooms with one of the other students and me. We had been playing around with some of the toys when he started to cry for whatever reason. I was blamed for the incident and was sent to the principal's office for punishment.

I was told to wait at the side until my name was called out and once it was, I was told to file in line with the other kids for my punishment. I believe the tool of the day was a yard stick. I had never been hit with one before, but when I saw the line of kids on the ground, it looked like a triage center where you put all your wounded kids. The only sound you could hear was the loud crying and the moaning! All I could think to myself was, wow! I'm standing in line waiting for this?

Several of the kids were lying on the ground with tears in their eyes because they had just been smacked by this yard stick; it looked like it really hurt! One by one the kids were falling like dominos…I was constantly thinking of a way to get myself out of this and I knew I had to do something and quickly.

Finally, I came up with a little scenario and my plan was for the principal! But how was I, a mere child, going to accomplish that? She was after all a short, plump little old lady sitting in a wheelchair and she had positioned herself at the right spot as to hit the kids with the yard stick. When my time had finally come, I got a close-up glimpse of a little girl who was right in front of me as she was getting a big whacking.

I felt like Bruce Banner, right before he changed into the Incredible Hulk! I could feel my breathing getting more and more shallow and my eyes grew wider with every stroke of the ruler, as it landing on her back side. As soon as the first whack hit her, a flood of tears instantly came rolling down her face.

You could see the shear pain from the yardstick; I was frozen right where I was standing and all I could do was stand there because of the sheer panic that inhabited that office. I could feel my rage building and it was only a matter of time before it had consumed me and changed me into the green monster.

After the little girl was done and was put down on to the floor with the other kids who were crying, it was my turn to step up to the plate and face the yardstick. My heart was racing a mile a minute and my body was starting to shake. I could feel my muscles starting to tighten up as I could feel my body start to take the shape of the Incredible Hulk.

I walked over to the principal, thinking there was no way I was going to take that kind of punishment from her. I had to do something and act fast. I did not want to feel the effects of getting whacked, especially because I, for once, did not actually do anything wrong. I stood looking around the office and in an instant I reacted.

I turned the table on her, and I felt myself reaching over her wheelchair and grabbing her yardstick out of her hand! My heart was racing, I was sweating, and my body was shaking all over! I had officially changed into the Hulk! I felt my body explode and I was releasing a rage of destruction down upon her!

Now she was the one who was getting smacked by the yardstick! I was letting it fly one after another hitting her back, left, and right. I was screaming out, "take that and that!" all the while having a smile on my face. Once I started whaling on her there was no going back because the minute I grabbed the yard stick out of her hand I was done at this school. It didn't matter to me because I hated it there anyway.

While all of this was going on, the teacher was staring in shock. I had just taken the ruler out of the principal's hand and was in the midst of dishing out some punishment to her in retaliation for hitting the other kids.

The children who were lying on the floor crying a short while ago had now gone silent; they couldn't believe I was beating the principal with that same yardstick. The entire office was so still, and I could feel everyone's eyes just staring at me. No one knew what to do.

But that didn't last long, as shortly thereafter one of the teachers pulled me off the principal and grabbed the yardstick out of my hands. If she hadn't, there was no telling how long I would have continued hitting the principal.

Once I was finally separated from the principal, I was pulled off to the side of the office with a couple of the teachers and they were asking me what was going through my mind. I didn't know what to say because I was still shaking. I just kept smiling at the teachers not saying a word. I looked back at the principal to see what kind of damage I had done to her and she was covered with bruises all up and down her entire body.

She was yelling and screaming, telling the other teachers to get me out of the office and to call my dad immediately to come pick me up. I was being expelled. The entire room was still completely silent; no talking from most of the teachers and no crying from any of the children. Everyone was still trying to wrap their heads around all that just happened.

After the principal finished looking over to see all of the bruises that had been bestowed upon her, she sent the kids out of the room and was still demanding that the teachers call my father immediately.

They called him several times and when one of the teachers finally got a hold of him, the principal demanded that she speak to him. Once she took the phone, the screaming at him began. All she said over and over again was, "You need to come pick up your son from class immediately because he was no longer wanted here!" When he asked why and what had happened, she explained that she would show him the results of my actions once he arrived. I was told by the principal to wait in a room by myself, in complete isolation, until he arrived.

While I waited for my dad to come and pick me up, I sat thinking about what had just happened, not saying a word. That moment of excitement would be the beginning of wanting to live life on the edge. I just sat and waited, smiling, until I was called back into the office.

Within a few minutes I was moved from isolation back into the principal's office, where I was told to think about my actions and the consequences which lie ahead. She kept going on and on about the whole thing until I eventually tuned her out.

I sat in her office for a good couple of hours and when my dad finally showed up, boy was he pissed! My first thought was what was he going to do to me? Was I going to get grounded? Get no play time outside or something even worse? I knew something had to be coming, but the more I sat listening to the conversation between them, she was the one getting the backlash. I couldn't believe it! I wasn't going to be in trouble? I listened for a while longer, amazed how he was talking about punishing the kids at school and he wasn't too thrilled about it either.

The shouting back and forth didn't last too much longer and after it was all settled, he told me to grab my stuff and go because we were done at this school. I quickly gathered my things and headed out the door. While I was walking to the car, I noticed some of the kids peeking out from behind the doors and looking out the windows smiling.

I smiled back at them while waving my final goodbyes, knowing that I would never see them again. Now it was on the other kids to deal with what had transpired.

Chapter Two

I was realizing that as I was getting older, I was starting to do things to see how far I could take them and exactly what I could get away with. But I was also realizing from the past instance, like with the principal, I was starting to like the "rush of excitement". I didn't know it at the time but I was slowly starting down a path to where I didn't care about the consequences of my actions.

Especially when it came to shoplifting. It didn't even matter what I was taking because the rush of excitement was more important to me than anything else. I could even honestly say that from childhood, shoplifting gave me a sense of joy in wanting excitement in my life. It was as if I was wanting attention from my parents but I didn't care what type of attention it was. It could be either good or bad but as long as it was some type of attention.

Even taking on some type of punishment from my actions when they were bad, gave me a sense of excitement in wanting to feel like I was alive and I didn't even care about the consequences.

The very first time I had ever taken something from a store was when I was about 9 years old and my older brother Jason had just entered the Boy Scouts. Our family had gone to the mall to buy what he needed. He was eager to get his uniform and all of the goodies that came along with it, like patches, buttons, and all other types of uniform pieces.

As he was trying on new uniforms in the dressing rooms, my parents were going back and forth getting the right sizes picked out. I had wandered off when my parents were not looking to see what I could get my hands on. My eyes were wondering when I saw this really cool Boy Scout patch and instantly, I knew I had to have it.

My body was starting to tremble with excitement, knowing that I had to take the patch. I could feel myself start to sweat from the anticipation! My heart felt like it was going to burst right out of my chest! It was perfect timing because my parents were paying attention to my brother, so I took the opportunity to grab the patch, put it in my pocket, and mingled around for a little while.

My body was still shaking from all the excitement and I knew I had to calm myself down before I got back to my parents.

Shortly after he was done trying on his uniforms, my parents called me over to the check-out counter where the cashier brought all of the uniforms and began putting everything into bags. Once everything was bagged up, we went through the mall to see what else he might need for the Boy Scouts.

As we started walking through the mall, I put my hands in my pocket for whatever reason. But I was not expecting what had happened next.

While my hand was in my pocket holding onto the patch, I walked a few more steps. My mom had stopped and accidentally bumped right into me. That movement made my hand shift out of my pocket while I was holding the patch, and suddenly the patch I had taken from the uniform shop flew out.

All I could see was the patch flying in the air as if it were in slow motion. I just stood there, watching, waiting for it to fall, and hit the ground. It was like time had come to a screeching halt and nothing else moved around except for the falling patch. As I stood there staring at the patch as it hit the ground, my dad saw what had come out of my pocket and he was in total disbelief. He couldn't believe I had just taken something from the store as they were shopping for my brother!

I tried to come up with some words to get out of it like "How did that get in my pocket"? But I knew instantly that it wasn't going to work. He then looked over to me, grabbed me by the shirt, walked over to a wall and asked where I had taken the patch from. I couldn't say anything even though I was still trying very hard to come up with a reason.

I was thinking of something along the line of "I found it on the ground," or "I don't know where it came from." I was even thinking like, "patch, what patch? I don't see any patch." I was a sitting duck at that point because I had been caught red handed. Nothing I was going to say would work. He asked me over and over again where I got it and I kept playing dumb over and over while repeatedly saying, "I found it on the ground while we walked out the store."

I held my ground and came up with excuse after excuse. All I could remember from that point was being dragged to the car while I was kicking and screaming. I knew what was in store for me as soon as I got home. My dad said, "Wait till we get home and I take out the metal spoon" Ah yes, Mr. Steel spoon. I had got to meet Mr. Steel spoon up close and personal one to many times already.

It was a spoon that had been handed down from my grandmother to him because it had also been used for some good punishments on my uncle while he was growing up.

I remember my grandmother telling me a story about when my uncle had done something wrong when he was a boy. She would always use a slotted steel spoon when she cooked and when she found out her son stole a nickel from one of his friends, the first thing she grabbed ahold of was that slotted spoon! She said she laid down a punishment he would never forget with that spoon to! More so she had smacked him on the butt so hard, that he had actually made a dented it! He had actually dented the steel spoon with his butt!

After all was said and done, she would still use that same spoon for many years to come to cook with and if need be, dishing out a punishment to anyone who acted up.

It had been used on me several times because of the stupid things I had done already at such a young age. That spoon had also become a psychological tool because of how many times it had been used on me. All he had to do was show me the metal spoon and tears would instantly flow out!

I could also say that at some point, the psychological aspect no longer made a difference to me. I had come to a point that with so many punishments, the effect of being smacked with the spoon had worn off. I mean how many times could I have been punished before it no longer made a difference? I had actually reached a condition to where I had to actually fake crying because the sensation of punishment no longer felt real.

It was as if my body and mind had become totally numb to facing any type of consequences from what my actions were doing. I did realize right from wrong and second guess myself every time I was going to do something that I wasn't supposed to. But the mere fact of feeling a sensation that made me feel more alive had outweighed any current consequences.

When we finally got back home, Dad went directly to the kitchen and was about to take the spoon out of the drawer and dish out my punishment. I knew what was coming but right before he had taken out the spoon, I finally had come clean and told him I had taken it from the store while they were getting Jason his uniforms.

I guess at that time I didn't want to drag this out anymore and just wanted to get this over with. I also knew my actions had consequences, but just the emotional thought of shoplifting had already given me what I wanted.

I had come to learn that since I had come clean, I would not be getting any type of punishment and would be off the hook for what I had just done with shoplifting. To me, those actions gave me what I wanted in getting my sense of excitement while admitting I had done something wrong. This had now given me a better sense of how I could use this to my advantage.

After I had admitted to my dad how I had taken that patch from the store, he decided that I was not going to be punished by Mr. Spoon but that I was going to be grounded for a while instead. Instantly I breathed a heavy sigh of relief! He told me to go to my room because I was going to be grounded for a while.

I gladly took that over the smacking from the spoon. Till this day my dad still cooks with that same spoon as a constant reminder of what had happened in the past.

Growing up with such strict parents made me feel that I needed more excitement in my life because I always felt like I was on a daily lockdown. I had to feel the need to experiment and at that point, the only way I could feel anything emotionally was doing something I was not supposed to do.

I knew I was different because I felt like I needed express myself constantly but I never could. I always felt awkward expressing my feelings because I always felt like I was going to get in trouble if I did. I guess you could say, I needed to push my boundaries every time I had the chance to because growing up in such a strict environment had suppressed so many emotions and growth.

More so, I couldn't see it or understand life back when I was a child but the mere fact that I needed to feel a sense of excitement, just to feel alive had also pushed me forward into being more self-destructive in so many ways.

Chapter Three

My father got a new job working in theatre and music production while living in San Bernardino, but the locations he would be working at were back in Orange County. This meant he would be doing a lot of commuting. He decided instead of doing countless hours of driving we would head back to Orange County, and the next city we settled in was Anaheim.

He wanted my brother and me to continue our education in a private school, so I started to attend a catholic school called Saint Justin's. It wasn't too bad in the beginning, but it was one of those types of schools where you had to follow what the nuns and priests said at all times or things could go bad really quick.

In order to pay for my brother's and my tuition, both my dad and mom were working full time. Mom was one of those people that always had to do something; she never wanted to just sit around and take time off because she felt that she always had to get up and move. Everywhere she went she walked, and it didn't matter if it was five blocks or fifteen blocks. It was always walking with her.

Everything I was learning I was absorbing like a sponge and over the next couple of years while I was at Saint Justin's, I would have many new and exciting experiences. I would be in all kinds of activities like flag football, the cub scouts, and track. I really got into track because every time I went running, I could the feel the excitement of running against other kids.

Especially when every time I crossed the finish line, I could feel my heart beating, my body would be shaking and all of my muscles were tensed up from all of the excitement! It never even mattered to me if I came in first or last place.

All I wanted to experience was the sensation of feeling alive and carefree every time I finished a race and I never wanted to come back down! This made the experience of running even greater because I felt I needed to keep pushing myself even more every time I ran.

I had reached the 4th grade and on one particular day, a new kid had just enrolled in school. He kept to himself a lot but was also the type of person who liked to show off all kinds of new toys and other things he brought with him to school.

While we were at recess, he had brought a couple of ninja stars to school and wanted to show them off to the other kids to see what they thought. It was more about him showing that he had weapons on school grounds. He had something that could do serious harm to someone and I couldn't keep my eyes off them.

I felt a sense of excitement as my body started to shake and my heart was pounding a mile a minute because *he had a weapon with him*, and now I wanted to join in the fun!

Now, for whatever reason, I had a nail clipper in my pocket and thought to myself, "how cool would it be if I pulled out the nail file and pretended it was a knife?" I took it out of my pocket and pulled out the file, exposing it as a knife. It worked because he actually thought I had a small knife in my hand while he had the ninja stars in his. As we were both talking, the bell rang for the end of recess and one of the kids on the playground ran over to where we were standing. He had seen that I had something in my hand and thought it looked really sharp. He then looked at me, saw the nail file along with the ninja star and in a blink of an eye, he ran off.

At first I thought he had gone away to play with some of the other kids, but I would find out shortly thereafter what he had actually done. Thinking nothing of it, I went back into the classroom and went back to my seat. Shortly after we all got settled, I heard my name called on the intercom to report to the principal's office immediately along with the name of the other kid who had shown me the ninja star.

I got up from my seat and went straight over to the principal's office. Sitting next to me in the waiting area was the boy who had come up to me, saw the nail file, and then turned around and ran off. I looked over at him and asked if he knew what this could be about. He looked at me and said he had no idea since he was called up to the office right before I was.

When his name was called, he went into the office and talked to the head nun for about 15 minutes and afterwards headed straight back to class without saying a word; he didn't even look at me as he left the office. "Wow," I thought. "That was really strange, what was all that about?"

Well to my surprise, when I was called into the office, I sat down next to the other boy who had the ninja stars. Ah Crap! I knew exactly what was happening! When the head nun started to talk, she asked me where the knife was that I had on the playground.

I immediately responded, "knife, what knife? I don't have any type of knife in my possession." She was getting really upset and raised her voice even louder and said, "The knife you were pointing at the other student on the playground!"

I sat for a few seconds taking it all in and then shouted out, "oooooooh you mean this nail file I have inside my pocket?" I took out the nail file and placed it on her desk showing her that's all it was. I realized this had all come down to where I was showing a nail file to a student at recess while another student ran up and saw that I was supposedly pointing a knife and I was about to stab him with it!

Once again, having an adrenaline rush got me in trouble. It was as if the universe was telling me that I needed to stop before life really got serious with adrenaline-experiences that would lead to more serious issues later in life.

No matter what I had said in trying to explain that it was only a nail file and all of the back-and-forth banter, it was still considered a weapon. I was told to stay seated in her office as she was going to call my father to come pick me up. I was being expelled for pointing a weapon at another student and threatening him with it! Believe it or not, I don't have many times in my life where I was actually innocent but this was one of those times where I was truly innocent of an accusation.

When my father finally arrived and saw me sitting in her office, he asked me what had happened. I told him I had brought a nail file to school and was showing another kid. It was sitting on her desk and when he saw that all it was is a nail file, he asked her what she thought it was after telling her it was a nail file.

She explained to him another student had run up to me at recess and thought I was about to attack him with it. He looked at her in utter amazement. He kept telling her over and over again it was only a nail file and there was nothing dangerous about it. She would hear nothing of it and didn't accept any of our explanations. He threw his hands up in the air and told her, "Ok, that's it!" He then told me to get my stuff from the classroom because we are done with this school.

Here we go again! Another school is down the drain.

I went back to the classroom, gathered my books, and went back up to the office without saying a word. I looked at the other kid who was in the office with the ninja stars and told him I hope nothing bad happens to him.

That would be the last time I would see him as we got in the car and drove off, never looking back.

Chapter Four

My dad decided enough was enough with the private schools. It was time to go into the public school system, so we picked an elementary school named Clara Barton. I would be there for 5th and 6th grades until I went into junior high.

During this time, a new type of trading card was getting really popular, called the Garbage Pail Kids. These cards were really a big hit and a very big-ticket item on the school grounds. At one point they were almost seen as a must have, meaning the more cards you had in your possession the more you wanted to collect them.

So, naturally, I did whatever I could to collect the most cards, I traded new toys for them, did homework for them, or even did favors for them, like helping someone clean their room or even as far as housework. It was crazy because I never wanted to clean up my own room but here I was, helping someone else clean up theirs for some trading cards! It's like they were made from money because of their tradability.

When class was being taught, I was literally working out a deal for a trade while the teacher was teaching her lesson and talking to the class. I totally ignored the lesson and kept on talking back and forth about a way I could trade for his cards. While whispering and working out a deal the teacher had overheard us talking and peaked over to see what we were doing. She then walked over to our desks and as she was getting closer, we tried to hide our cards from her sight by stuffing them inside our desks, but without success.

She came over and stood right in front of us, put her hand out and asked us to hand them over to her. Reluctantly, we looked at each other, collected them and put them in her hand. I intently watched where she was going to put them and while she walked over to a closet, she opened the door, put them inside the cabinet and locked them up.

She then turned towards us and said that we would not be getting them back until the end of the school year because we were doing something in class that we were not supposed to be doing. My face dropped and I said back to the teacher, "Till the end of the school year? That's a long time to wait for them!"

With that in mind, the other student and I formulated a plan to get our cards back. Our plan was that we would wait until recess so we could sneak back into the classroom and take our cards from out of the closet.

As we put our plan together, I was looking around inside the classroom to see if I could find a way to get back inside once we were out to recess. I noticed there was a back door which was used in case of emergency, but the teacher always had the door open from time to time.

It so happened to be one of those hot summer days when she would leave the door open, but for safety reasons, every recess the door was to be closed and locked to make sure no one got back inside the classroom.

During the recess period I had volunteered to close the back door and make sure it was locked before everyone left the classroom. My next step was to put a pencil at the bottom of the door so it was cracked slightly which made it an easy entry way to get back into the classroom. When everything was all set and the bell rang for everyone to go outside for recess, we both snuck around to the back door of the classroom, opened the door where I had put the pencil and went inside the classroom.

My heart was racing a mile a minute! Instantly the palms of my hands were sweating! My body was shaking with all of the excitement I was feeling! It's as if I could hear a pin drop because all of my senses had instantly been heightened.

Sneaking into the classroom knowing it would mean big trouble if we got caught, but at that point in time I didn't care or think about the consequences. All that mattered was getting my cards back. We tried to find the key that would open the closet door but had no such luck so we looked around to find something that would fit inside the lock.

The next best thing that we could come up with was a pair of scissors, so I quickly grabbed them, put them inside the lock and tried to shake the door open for several minutes, but the lock was just too stubborn for us. We tried everything we could to open the cabinet door but to no avail, so we left the classroom through the back door, closed it up and locked it. We went back out to the playground dejected but still thinking of ways we could get the cards out of the closet and possibly try it again soon.

As the bell rang for us to go back into the classroom, we all went back inside, sat down, and continued our schoolwork for about an hour, until all of a sudden the other student and I were called into the principal's office. We both immediately got up from our chairs and started our walk up into the hallway thinking about why we were summoned there.

When we got to her office, we were told to wait there until the principal was ready to talk to us. Thoughts kept racing through my head as to why we were there in the first place. After about 20 minutes we were each called into the office separately for a one-on-one discussion with the principal, and I was first to appear. She told me to sit down, and she would explain everything to me in full detail. She started out by saying that my father was on his way up for a visit. "Wait my father?" I asked? "What would he be coming here for?"

The principal then proceeded to tell me she had found out what I and the other student had done. I looked at her in total amazement, as if I had no idea what she was talking about, and asked, "What did we do?"

She stared back at me for a couple of seconds and said that we both had broken into the classroom, for starters, and then tried to take something back which had been locked up in the closet. I sat speechless! How did she find all this out? Was someone listening to what we were doing? Did someone see us sneak into the classroom? I didn't want to believe she had found out what we had done.

While all of the talking was going on back and forth, my father was sitting outside in the hallway waiting to be called inside the office. He had the look of death on his face and was just waiting to give me an ass whooping!

There was always something about my dad in the way he hid his emotions and anger. For his entire life, he always wore these dark sunglasses so you could never see his eyes. You could never see what he was really looking at or what he was really thinking. He could be looking at you or someone else around you. But that was his point, keeping his eyes out of sight.

He also had this scowl on his face that almost never changed, even when he tried to smile, his face still bent towards the sour puss face, add that, along with the sunglasses, gave him one of the best all-time poker faces that anyone has ever seen.

After seeing the look on his face while he walked into the office, he asked what the problem was. The principal slowly went into saying what had just happened while the class was out in recess. She said I and another student had broken into the classroom and tried to steal back my cards out of a locked cabinet.

He stared at me for a couple of seconds because he couldn't believe what he was hearing. The only words that came out of his mouth were, “Lock him up and take him away.” He then quickly turned around and proceeded to walk out the front door! I was in total disbelief! He just kept walking and didn’t turn around until the principal called him back into the office. Even the principal just sat there staring at me in shock because she had never seen a reaction like that before from a parent.

I just sat there with tears rolling down my eyes saying, “No! No! I won’t do it again!”

She told me to settle down and then talked to him explaining what was going to happen next. I was automatically suspended for 3 days and had to pay for any damages that were caused. Lucky for us, when we tried and failed to get the lock open, we stopped, which prevented any damage to the classroom or the cabinet doors, so no damages had to be paid out.

After a lengthy discussion, she explained everything to us and said I was suspended effective immediately and needed to go home right then and there. I walked out of the office with tears still rolling down my face. I looked with sadness at the other boy sitting and waiting outside the principal’s office for his turn. We made eye contact briefly and he immediately went into panic mode too, after he saw what had just happened to me.

I told him that I would see him in a couple of days and he knew exactly what I was saying. He was now buying his time until his dad showed up to talk to the principal. My dad and I walked to the car and not a word was spoken until we got home.

When we got back home he dialed up my Grandmother on the phone and talked to her for about 30 minutes. He told me to go to my room and said, "You're really lucky that nothing was broken in that classroom, or this could have been a lot worse."

I still didn't say a word and just hid out until he was done talking to her. He didn't do anything drastic except say I was grounded for the next three days and I couldn't do anything while I was on suspension except stay in my room and make myself busy.

After the three days were up, I went back to school as if nothing had ever happened, except for all the whispers and chatter from the other kids about how we had broken into the classroom a couple of days ago. As quickly as the chatter went around about the break in, it was quickly overshadowed by something even bigger.

Apparently, word had got around to the other grade levels, on how easy it was to get inside one of the classrooms. It so happened that while I was suspended, one of the sixth-grade classrooms had been broken into and vandalized costing several thousand dollars in damages to it.

I thought to myself, was this the start of something bad? I hoped it wasn't because of what I had already been through and didn't want to hear any more about it.

Several days later, it was officially announced that those who had vandalized the classroom were caught because they wanted to top what we had done. I know it's hard to justify that I was just trying to get my cards back, compared to what others had done for the shear destruction of the classroom. They figured since we did it, it would be easy for everyone else to break in and that no one would find out.

We were told they were so brash that they even walked out of the classroom with the computers and took them home! I asked what had happened to them, they were expelled immediately and their parents had to pay for all of the damage to the classroom which turned out to be pretty expensive.

The main kicker was after it was all done, the school pressed full charges and they all had to spend some time in juvenile hall because of how serious the damage was. They were slapped with a felony along with it. That was a real serious lesson for me to learn and I told myself from here on in I was done with doing stupid things…or so I thought.

Our 6th grade class was making plans for a small ceremony held inside the classroom. I can't remember exactly who brought it up or how it all started but someone had suggested that we should play a prank on the teacher on the last day of class.

A prank huh? This sounded like it could be fun! After all, what was the worst that could happen? It's not like anyone is going to get hurt, so I totally bought into it. We had all come up with the idea of doing a small magic show and would have some balloons along with some other items. What we were going to put inside the balloons was going to be the prank. But before we could do anything, we had to run it by the teacher first so we could get her approval.

We got the approval and started our plan. The day before we had the graduation ceremony, we ran the magic show idea by the teacher and explained to her what we were going to do. We made a plan for the show, but it was all an act because we were never going to follow through with them anyway; it was all just a front until the real magic started after the ceremony.

Each of us had a part; mine was going to be the grand finale because my prank was going to be with balloons. Specifically, the balloons were going to be filled with shaving cream and water.

When the day came, and right after the ceremony ended, the show started right up. The others were doing some silly stuff entertaining the class.

My part had finally come, it was show time! I had directed the teacher to a chair which was placed in front of the classroom and told her to sit down with her face towards the middle of the class. I then told her to close her eyes and not to open them no matter what she was hearing around her. Once she sat down and closed her eyes, I stood behind her and opened my backpack while the other kids were talking to her so as to distract her from hearing anything. I got my backpack open, pulled out the balloons and sat them on the ground. Everyone in the class was starting to get louder and louder once they saw all the balloons. I had to do the trick fast because my body was tensing up from all of the excitement!

Once I had the balloon in my hand, my body started to shake frantically! I could feel my heart pound as if it wanted to jump outside of my body! I didn't know which I liked more, the anticipation of doing the prank or doing the actual prank. I was so filled up with excitement, I felt as if I could burst!

I yelled out to the class, "Are you ready for your show?!"

Everyone yelled back "Yes!"

Before I knew it, I took a balloon with the shaving cream in my hand and popped it on the teacher's head! I then picked up a water balloon and tried to pop it so the water would come out, but no matter how hard I tried, the balloon wouldn't pop.

Overall, I guess it was a good thing because as she felt the shaving cream, she stood up immediately and shouted out, "Enough! This ends now!" We all stood there not saying a word because after all, what could we really say? We had been caught playing a prank on the teacher instead of doing a magic show for the class.

When she got up from the chair, she looked at all of us and demanded we go back to our seats and sit down, but as I was walking back to my seat, she grabbed my backpack and looked inside. She found a few other water balloons inside the bag and kept them at her desk because she was going to take them up to the principal. When she stood up in front of the class talking to everyone that was involved with the magic show, she directly looked at each one of us and said how disappointed she was in our actions. There wasn't much we could do from that point except to remain silent.

After the stern talking to, the class was quiet for the rest of the day, and once the final bell rang for our grade completion, we all filed out of the classroom one by one.

While we were all leaving as quickly as we could move, our teacher let us know that once we left the classroom, she was going to go up to the principal's office and let him know about the prank. She also said our parents were going to be notified as to what had happened with the prank and every little detail.

We all walked out of the class and went our separate ways. I didn't think too much of it because my body was still shaking and my heart was still pounding. It didn't matter because I was still on cloud nine, not even thinking about what had just happened.

My parents, on the other hand, were pissed!

As soon as I got home, I was sent right to my room and was done for the rest of the day. I don't recall exactly what happened after the prank, but I eventually came down from all the excitement and it slowly sank in about what I had done. Just the thought of what I had done with a "supposed prank" sent shivers down my spine.

I was slowly realizing what my impulses were doing to me and how quickly things could get out of control. These sudden impulses were quickly leading me down a path of self-destruction and doing some really, really stupid things.

Chapter Five

Shoplifting and the sense of excitement had never seemed to stop for me. Not only grabbing popular toys, but also everything else I possibly could get my hands on. Every time we went shopping, I'd always come out of the store with something, even if it was the most mundane item.

My dad was constantly telling me stories, ones I had no idea ever existed that I started stealing things at a very early age. Even before I could walk and sitting in the shopping cart. He said I would reach across the aisle grab, grab an item, and put my pocket.

Sometimes as we walked around the malls and went inside the stores, I would see something sitting there on a shelf and it didn't even have to be something I wanted or needed. At times I would even toss the item in question in the trash as soon as I got out of the store. I didn't give much thought to the possibility of getting caught and I didn't actually care about what I took. Eventually my room filled up with so many useless items. The more I saw kids at school with something new, the more I desired to beat the other kids in getting something that was a lot better than what they had. It wasn't even about the toys; it was the excitement of constantly getting something new.

At first, my older brother never really knew where I was getting all these toys. Most of the time when I came home, I would have something new. He would ask where I got all the toys and I explained to him that I was always trading up for them while I was at school. After a while, he started to catch on to my schemes. Often, he would see items that made no sense and seemed to be of little interest to me. So, I told him the next time we went out to the shopping center, I would show him how I was getting away with all the goodies.

One afternoon, when our dad needed to go shopping, we piled into the car and ended up going to a place called Gemco. When we walked through the doors, I told my dad we were going to look at the new toys in the toy section and my brother and I quickly ran off into the toy aisle to see what was new.

I browsed around and saw a cool GI Joe figure that I *had* to have. Naturally, I showed my brother how I took the figure out of the package, put it in my pocket and would head back to find our parents, like it was an everyday event.

He asked, "That's all there was to it?"

It was that easy, at least for the time being. So, after we got home and unpacked the car, I showed him all of the figures I had "collected" over the last few trips to the store. Amazed and impressed with everything I had accumulated, he now wanted to start a collection like mine.

Every time I went back to school after going shopping, I was showing off on the playground everything I had just taken from the store. Not only was it a rush trying to outdo everyone else with something new every time, but it was also a thrill to be at the top with having the latest and the coolest new toys!

As I said, my brother now wanted to get some of the toys, so the next time we went to Gemco, he wanted to get something along with me. Being the kid with all the cool toys also excited him.

The following weekend we went back to Gemco, and as we entered the store, we ran off to the toy isle to see what new toys they had hanging up. My brother saw an action figure he *had* to have. I told him I would take the figure and he would take the rest of the pieces. For some reason he kept frantically moving around the isle. I don't know if it was because he was nervous or what it was, but as he was darting all over the place. He entered an area where there were these big silver mirrors up above all the aisles. I had never noticed them until that day.

I didn't know it at the time, but they were those one-way mirrors which you can only look out but could not look back in and see what was behind the mirror. My brother continued to move around the aisle and his walking eventually took us right to the front of the mirror, and before I knew it we were in the dead center of the mirrors.

All I can remember was looking up at the mirror, staring straight into them and seeing my reflection, not even knowing why these mirrors where up there to begin with. I also didn't know it at the time, but that was the main security office for the entire store and a security officer was always looking down on everyone behind the mirrors.

I started to feel a bit nervous about the mirrors and told him to hurry up because we had to get back to the cart before they thought we were doing something wrong. So, we quickly filled our pockets and ran back to find our parents.

Eventually, we found or parents walking down one of the food aisle and we quickly grabbed onto the shopping cart. I was feeling a bit anxious and wanted to get out of the store. The thought of getting caught was starting to enter my mind. My chest was pounding! I could feel all of the blood rushing through my veins; it was an awesome feeling for just a split second and I kept telling myself everything was going to be good and there was nothing to worry about.

Boy was I wrong!

While we were checking out and getting the bags put into the shopping cart, I looked around the store several times and noticed a tall man, thin mustache over his lip, dressed in jeans and a checkered long sleeve shirt with a vest. We started to walk out, and I turned around to see him following us while looking away.

As we started to walk towards the exit door, I noticed him closing in behind us. Each time I looked around to see where he was, he gave me a stare for a couple of seconds and then he would turn away and act like nothing was wrong.

I didn't think too much of it at that time and figured he was just taking a look around the store or that he was just some weirdo. But the closer we came to the exit, the closer he got. Now my nerves were on edge; something was seriously wrong. I was getting all shaky and my heart was now pounding even faster than before!

Once we approached the exit door, there was no turning back; we just crossed that line and were now standing outside the shopping center. The man who had been following us closed in quickly. He turned his head and the first thing I heard out of his mouth was, "Excuse me sir. I need to ask you a couple of questions."

As he was looking directly at my dad, he reached right into his pocket, pulled out a security badge and asked us to step back into the store. I couldn't move, standing frozen in my tracks.

We had just been caught red handed.

My dad's face had that "stare of death," it was as if his eyes could pierce right through you and turn your insides out and melt your soul! It was even worse because he was wearing his dark sunglasses, which hid his eyes and you couldn't see who he was looking at. The security officer told us we needed to follow him upstairs for some questioning and he wanted to find out exactly what we had just done.

We followed him upstairs, sat down, and he then started to ask me questions like, "How many times have you done this? Where is the package? Where are all of the pieces for the toys?" He then looked at my brother and started to ask him some of the same questions, but my brother couldn't even get out a word because he broke down and went totally silent. He couldn't even look at the security guard because of his horror of getting caught.

We gave the security officer the answers he wanted to hear and told us we were not going to be arrested because it was just an action figure and they recovered all of the pieces. But the main punishment was we were never allowed to go back into that store because of the shoplifting code, which barred us from ever returning. That was fine with my brother and me, but our dad was not very pleased. And that is an understatement!

As we finished and got up from our chairs, the security officer walked us out the front door and we headed straight for the car, got inside, and drove back home. Our dad didn't say a word the entire way back and you could see the steam coming off his head because he was really pissed and couldn't believe what he had just been put through, all because of our antics.

Once we finally got home, he told us to put the food away and go to our room. We looked at each other, walked to our room and now we awaited our sentencing.

Dad calmed down for a little bit and then went to call our grandmother and after about an hour of talking to her, he came into the room and said that she wanted to talk to me. She explained to me that she had to calm him down because he was about to put us through the wall! She asked if I had learned my lesson, but for whatever reason I hesitated for a couple of seconds because I wanted to know where this was going.

She repeated the same question, and I still hesitated to answer her because, after all, did I learn my lesson? Was I going to give up all of the other possibilities of getting my all-important adrenaline fix? I finally answered yes, I had learned my lesson and she responded very firmly that this had better not happen again. I then gave the phone back to my dad.

I stood there for a couple of seconds because I had just lied to my grandmother! I couldn't believe that I told her I was sorry for what I had done, but in reality, I wasn't the least bit sorry.

I was actually ready to go back to the store, learn from my mistakes and do it all over again the right way without getting caught, not so much for the toys, but for feeling alive! My brother on the other hand learned his lesson quickly, and from then on, he never touched a thing at any store without paying for it. I guess it is true that the type of people you choose to have in your life can influence you and your decisions.

I turned this page as a life learning experience and never wanted to make those mistakes again.

Chapter Six

Once I moved on into junior high, I was constantly looking for new and different ways of pushing my boundaries. One of the biggest things to do while growing up in the latch key kid era was skateboarding; everyone at the time was riding skateboards or had a BMX bike.

My brother and I had an uncle who worked at a skateboard factory called *Powell Peralta*, and we were always getting great equipment and accessories straight from the factory. We always had new skateboards, tee shirts, stickers, or just about anything that was new that our uncle would send out to us. It was a little bit of a rush making a little bit of cash on the side, selling the skateboard products to other skaters.

I loved the idea of jumping over people with a skateboard, but even more exciting was jumping off rooftops and landing on the sidewalk standing on top of my deck. It was exactly what I was looking for with the added factor of danger, which challenged me to do more wild tricks.

It was an exhilarating experience, but one which didn't last too long because I eventually needed something new. There were only so many roof tops I could jump off of at that time and after a while they all seemed the same. Skateboarding wasn't cutting it anymore and wasn't giving me what I needed. As quickly as the skateboard fad reached its height, it blew by with something entirely different and I needed to find the new, "X factor."

Any teenager will tell you that trends change all of the time. One day you can have the coolest thing or wearing the trendiest new clothes, and the next day, poof, the trend had now shifted into something completely different. You always want to keep up with the fads and what was popular around the school.

One of the newest trends was taking car hood ornaments and making them into a key chains. Hood ornaments? I thought, "Really? This was the new trend everyone was talking about?" I didn't know how or why, but one day someone at school brought a hood ornament on campus for giggles and instantly, it was all the rage.

Of course, the better the car the better the ornament, and everyone took notice. You should have seen everyone's eyes looking at this thing; it was a Mercedes Benz hood ornament and had a very high shine to it. The ornament was also gold plated so you knew it came from a cool looking car.

There was no stopping anyone or this craze at that point because kids were making good money for those things; they were actually shelling out cash to buy these hood ornaments! In fact, that gold one went for $50.00, and the silver ones went for about $25.00. It came down to the fact that this was sure to be a short-term fad and you wanted to get as many of them as possible and get as much money as possible before the craze ran out. In a short period of time, kids demand for them grew, and the best ones from high end cars were selling like hot cakes.

Everyone wanted in on it!

Realizing how crazy everyone was for these key chains and how much they were willing to pay, I knew I had to get my hands on as many hood ornaments as possible and as quickly as possible while everyone was still wrapped up in the current fad. It seemed like if you didn't have one, you were not recognized as part of the *in* crowd, but for me, it was all about the quick cash that I wanted to make.

I came up with a plan that myself and a friend of mine would go out on a spree and hunt down as many hood ornaments as we possibly could. We would go up and down each neighborhood street trying to locate the higher end cars like the Mercedes and the Cadillacs because they were the most prized, commanding the most money.

Night after night we went out searching, until we couldn't find any more in our neighborhood. We made some good money at school selling them to the kids who were willing to pay and taking this as far as we possibly could.

The demand was ever growing and some of the kids were willing to pay a bit more to have the gold-plated ornaments, which kept me going out for a few more nights.

I had finally found what I was looking for!

It may have been only a short while, but I was going to enjoy every minute of it! I was starting to really like what I was experiencing, and just as before, it wasn't even about the money I was making.

It was truly about the excitement and the danger of stealing the ornaments and the distinct possibility of getting caught. But since a lot of the cars already had their ornaments taken, I wanted to change things up and get them while the sun was out. It carried a lot more risk, but I thought the reward would make up for it with our little adventure. I told another friend of mine we should try to "lift" these hood ornaments right in the middle of the day without getting caught.

So, the next morning we were on the hunt, and the first car we pulled up to was an old Cadillac sitting in the parking lot next to a cargo truck. Immediately I started to feel my heart race! My mind was all dialed in and time had felt like it was at a standstill. This time around I was pushing new boundaries, which made this moment even more exciting! I was really amped up and ready to go, so I pulled out the wire cutters and pulled back the hood ornament.

Suddenly the driver from inside the car jumped up from the driver's seat!

His car seat was reclined all the way back, and apparently he was sleeping in the car for whatever reason and I don't know why I didn't peak inside the car at first. I was thinking that the car was sitting there as the owner was at work. When he popped up from the car seat, he scared the living hell out of me and as he jumped up from the seat and started to open the door, my friend yelled out, "Move it! Peddle, Peddle!"

The man jumped out of the car and started to run after us! I never peddled so hard in my life! Quickly I turned around to see how close he was, but after a couple of minutes he had slowed down and eventually gave up chasing us.

I had pushed my luck to the limit and from that point on, I was finished with the hood ornament fad and would move on to something else. My number had been called and my luck had officially run out. More so, I was not feeling the excitement of this adventure.

It was a good time with it while it lasted.

Ultimately the guy running after me was a true sign that I needed to move on and put that whole ordeal behind me.

Jason and I skateboarding in the early 1980's

Chapter Seven

Just like with my 6th graduation, going from grade school into junior high, our middle school class was in the process of having a small graduation before moving on to high school.

While doing some pre-graduation rehearsals, one of the kids spoke about possibly playing a prank at the graduation ceremony to make it more entertaining. This time around, I didn't want anything to do with it since the last one for grade school was a total failure. But the spur of the moment excitement had always pulled me back in.

One would think that the thought of *here we go again* would have made me want to hold back. However, knowing my past with pranks and the trouble that came with them, I couldn't stop myself; I wanted to be counted in. Once that thought got into my head, there was no turning back.

We had talked about bringing some paint balls along with some other crazy items that would make a huge mess during the ceremony.

Graduation day was approaching fast and I needed to get some paint balls while the other two kids got the other items. I don't want to go too much into details, but it was going to be epic!

A few days earlier, my mom had given me some money for some graduation clothes and I had purchased a brand-new outfit. Little did I know I would not be wearing it for too long at the ceremony.

When graduation day arrived, we were getting prepared for the prank and went over how we were going to proceed, when a female student walked by and overheard us talking about our plan. She quickly ran off and told the nearest teacher exactly what she had heard.

It was de je vu all over again! My thoughts went back to 6th grade graduation with the magic show.

Immediately the teacher came over and asked us to empty our pockets and backpacks and to lay everything out on the ground. Of course, she wanted an immediate explanation. We were all quiet except for one friend who cracked and gave everything up.

She couldn't believe what we were about to do and instantly expelled us right there on the spot, meaning we were not allowed to do our walk at the ceremony. She told us to wait there while she called the principal over.

When the principal grabbed everything we had brought, we were dismissed from our graduation and told to leave the premises. All I could do was pick up my backpack and head out. I got my bike from the bike rack and rode around the streets for a couple of hours, wasting time until the graduation ended and then headed home like everything was ok.

When I got home my parents asked how graduation went. I told them everything had gone great without any problem. They both just stared at me.

"Really? No problems huh?"

My dad asked me if anything else happened while I was at school. I acted like nothing was wrong, but I was wondering where he was going with this. After all, he wouldn't be asking me that question if everything was good. I told them I was headed to my room to change.

My dad said, "Good, why don't you stay in there for a while and think about what you did." That was it, he officially knew what had happened. I didn't know it at the time but, while I was on my way back home, the principal had called my parents' house and informed him that I was expelled from the graduation. and was sent home.

"Oh boy!" I thought to myself as the blood drained from my face; I was caught once again. I thought I had dodged a bullet but I was already busted while I was on my way back home. He looked at me and said, "Your grounded indefinitely."

Once again, another crazy spur of the moment plan for that intoxicating life moment had taken me down the well beaten path of trouble and punishment.

Chapter Eight

Going into high school, I knew life was going to be a whole new experience. While others were more worried about their schoolwork, sports, or whatever else drove them, I was always driven by having a good time, the excitement of the unknown, and making money the quickest way possible. I was not really into the whole school thing from the beginning because I found it quite boring. The wheels in my mind were always turning in search of new and daring ways of excitement.

I was on the lookout for the next fad that would bring me some extra cash and I found it in comic books, more specifically, Batman, which was out in the movie theaters, as well as sports cards. Collectable comics were all over the place and many kids were heavily into it; I was one of those kids who was hooked. I had to have comics in my hands because they were a hot commodity and could be sold quickly. Every weekend when I was at a different comic store, I would buy a comic and get a couple more for free.

Instantly I would then turn around and sell them to the kids at school. I developed an obsession of getting the most out of every store visit just to see how many comics I could get without paying for them. Everywhere I went, I stole as many comics as possible. I would visit several stores as often as I could and come out with stacks of them every time. I would look around the store to make sure no one was watching, then lift up the front of my shirt and slide them in my shorts.

Most of the time, I would grab two of the same comics to use one of them as a buffer. More so, use the duplicate comic as a protector against my body so the other ones don't stick to me from all the sweat. More than anything, I was also getting that crazy rush.

Comics were good for a short while, but on the other side, sports cards were making their way into the school, and many kids had not collected them for years. It was right when the Batman fad had fizzled out that collecting sports cards had taken over. High school sports were always a huge thing and many teenagers wanted to try to relate to the sports they were also playing.

It was just like old times when I was in elementary school collecting the Garbage Pail Kids cards. But his time around, sports cards were the main collectible and lots of the other grades were really into collecting them too. Our campus even had a sport card club after school so you could join and learn about the other types of sports and see what they had to offer.

I quickly jumped over into card collecting and had amassed quite a collection, just the same way I did as the comics in stealing as many as I could. I needed to amass as big as collection as I could and since I didn't have much money at the time, the best alternative was go to as many retailers as I could and steal as many cards as possible.

I would then sell them off quickly to other students on campus for a nice quick profit. In my mind, it was a win, win! I didn't pay any money for the cards and in turn, made a lot of money on the side by selling them!

For the time being, I was making some good money with the comics and sports cards. Eventually this was going to change with a newer fad and I had to find the next thing. The idea of getting a job was out of the question for me because it would have taken away from my free time. So, I was primed and ready for what was coming next.

Money was good in selling collectibles, especially with getting a constant rush with stealing, but now my body and mind was craving more. Now I wanted to go bigger and better and get more excitement out of what I was doing!

I actually had a couple of knives hidden around in my bedroom. I acquired them from others that I knew, mostly because they wanted me to hold onto them for a short while. Never asking why or any questions, I just simply stashed them away.

In the long run, the people who I held them for never asked for them back, for whatever reason, so I simply kept them and stashed them way until I decided what to do with them. I knew I could sell them off to anyone who was willing to buy them and decided to poke around on campus and see.

I had brought a switchblade and butterfly knife to one of my early classes and asked around the class to see if anyone was interested in buying them. Within a few of minutes, I found a couple of students who were interested in buying them! I named my price and boom! Cash was in my hands and the knives were in theirs! I was intrigued by how much money I had just made compared to what I as getting for the collectibles. This was it! My new sense of excitement was now going to come from selling weapons on campus!

Just as I had sold the knives, one of the students who I had someone to had asked me if I was able to get my hands on any firearms. That question instantly stopped me in my tracks because

I didn't know how to answer it. Knives were one thing, but guns were on a whole different level! I had told him I would ask around and see what I could come up with.

To make it even more enticing, the student who wanted to buy the gun said he would pay me 500.00 cash for it. "Um, 500.00" I repeated back to him. He said "Yes" and that he would have it the day I brought it to him. I started to sweat and my body started to shake wildly! The thought of making 500.00 in a single day was far too much to pass up on.

Over the next couple of days, I had asked a couple close friends of mine if they knew anyone who had any contact with getting any firearms. One friend in particular named Tran, mentioned he was in the process of selling one to a student on campus and at lunch time, he wanted to show me what he was selling.

Wait, I thought, he actually brought one of them to campus in his car?

When lunch time came around, I went out to his car to see what he had brought. Sitting there in the back of his car was a handgun with two extra clips loaded with full rounds in them. Holy crap, this dude brought a gun onto campus! Tran picked up the gun and mentioned how much money he was getting for the sale. When Tran told me he could get more of them and that they were an easy sell to the other kids, it was a total shock because who the hell sells guns to other teens? It's not like this was a comic book or even sports cards! These were loaded weapons!

But the more important question I had was, who in their right mind would actually have that kind of cash to buy one of these? Tran told me the reason he brought this specific gun was it had already been sold to another student and he was there to collect the funds.

I thought, "Damn!! Already sold?"

I knew this was the route I wanted to take! My body and mind instantly went into a whirl wind of excitement! The high I was feeling at that point in time was the best I had felt in a very long while. The raw emotions and sensations I was feeling meant, I didn't care about any of the consequences that may come from these transactions. I only cared about that brief moment of excitement and ecstasy that I would be feeling from getting the weapons and making the sale. I didn't even care that I would be selling them on school grounds, or for that matter, who I would be selling them too!

Quickly snapped back to reality and was now turning out the possibilities of what I could make as far as cash goes. Tran also mentioned he was always looking for new routes in getting new and different weapons and if I knew anyone who could supply them, they could get a nice pay day. Or for that matter, even connecting him with someone who wanted to buy a weapon, Tran was willing to pay a finder's fee for the transaction.

After he left, I stood for a moment taking this all in. These guns brought everything to a whole new level, but on the other hand was the thought of all the damage one of the shots could do to someone. This was a totally different avenue which could hurt someone or even kill them!

Unfortunately, my logic wasn't winning because, after all, it had always come back to the money and the excitement of doing something dangerous. Just the thought of the raw danger form what could happen made my body tense up, my head spin around with a sense of ecstasy, my eyes widen as big as possible and my legs shake with every moment that passed by.

Eventually, I decided I was all in on the weapons and was now transitioning into something way out of my comfort zone. Any amount of money I would be making would far exceed anything I had done before. To me, I was all in no matter what the consequences would lead to.

I had finally made a contact with Tran and brought in him with the student who was looking to buy a gun. I didn't know what to say at first, but I quickly shifted Tran over to him and introduced them to each other. After they finished talking, they both went their separate ways and Tran mentioned that I would have some cash waiting for me once this as all wrapped up.

He got his weapon in a matter of days and once I saw Tran, he handed me a 100.00 dollar bill! A 100 bucks! Just for getting them together and selling a gun! “This was all way too easy” I thought. I was getting extra money on the side but more importantly, the sense of excitement made it even more worth wile.

Chapter Nine

I was constantly asking around others on campus for any possible connections to any type of weapon. I was talking out loud one day and my brother Jason overheard my conversation. He knew someone in one of his classes named John, who had access to all kinds of guns and knives because his dad owned a gun shop. A perfect situation!

Over the next couple of weeks, I got to know John really well and would go over to his house after school. More so, I wanted to see what kinds of weapons he had around his house. The very first time I walked in, my eyes bulged out of my head! Stashed all over the living room and kitchen, were handguns, knives, and ammunition!

I thought to myself, I hit the mother lode of a weapons trove! My body was trembling with excitement! I could hardly breathe because my body had locked itself up with all of the excitement and with the thoughts of 100.00 dollar bills dancing around inside my head! I asked John if he was willing to trade or give any of the stuff away. He was a big comic book collector and was willing to trade comics for anything that I wanted.

Bingo! I now had an inside track! I knew that I could make more money selling weapons to students then I could selling them comic books. I quickly started off small by getting some bullets for the firearms and bringing them back home, along with some different types of knives. This way I would have something ready to sell as I picked them up one at a time.

Every trip I made to his house gave me a sense of wonder and enjoyment. I knew that the more comics I traded with John, the more money I was going to make in the long run. I was going to ride this ecstasy and sense of excitement for as long as I possibly could.

I had put the word out in my first period class that I now had personal access to different types of weapons. A student named Julio came up to me and mentioned he was looking to buy a gun and was willing to pay $500.00 for it. I told him I would see what I could find and would bring it to class once I got my hands on it.

I quickly went over to John's to see what he had hidden around the house. I didn't want to take anything that was out in the open since that would make things obvious to those living inside the house. One gun instantly had caught my eye. It was a chrome plated .45 auto magazine that really stood out and it was exactly what I wanted! I picked up the gun and stood silently looking over the entire weapon. My body started to shake and my knees started to quiver! I was now holding an instrument in my hand that can instantly kill someone.

Just the thought of the raw power I was holding made me want to keep it all to myself and not want to sell it. I had never felt any emotion or feeling like this before. The idea of me holding an instrument of destruction gave me a feeling of empowerment and that I can take a person's life just by pulling that trigger.

I didn't want that moment to end because of what I was feeling but I knew Jason and I had to quickly leave. We ended up taking the gun and putting it in my backpack and left John's house. My brother and I jumped on our skateboards and skated off back home as fast as we could.

We were both laughing because we had taken a gun together and from the money we were going to make, it seemed like the perfect caper.

I didn't know it at the time, but the gun was actually loaded with a fifteen round magazine and had a round in the chamber. With all of the emotions I was feeling when I was holding the gun, I didn't even know it was loaded! I was lucky that something didn't hit the trigger and make the gun go off in my backpack killing me or someone else!

As we pulled up to the house, Jason and I went into our bedroom and took the gun out of my backpack. Jason wanted to hold it but wanted to make sure that nothing happened to either of us. So, he took the round out of the chamber and took out the clip to not set anything off.

After we both sat there looking at it for a few minutes, I stashed it underneath my bed so I could plan on what I was going to do with it.

With the $500 Julio was going to give me, I was now going to be able to buy all of the baseball cards I had been wanting. All I had to do was get the gun to him and collect the cash. The fact that I was selling a gun to another student didn't bother me one bit! It was all about the adrenaline rush of selling the gun and bringing it on campus. This, undoubtedly, would be huge and the cash was just what I needed.

After finalizing the deal with Julio, I agreed to bring the gun the next day and we would settle everything up. I arrived at school extra early just to get my thoughts together. It's funny because I never came to class on time and would always stroll in late. This would be the only moment I ever did because of what I was about to do.

Excited with anticipation and I decided to walk around campus for a little bit. I had to find a way to get rid of the extra adrenaline in my body because it was fogging up my mind and I needed to get my thoughts in order. I quickly walked around some of the classrooms to tire myself out a bit, but there was no such luck because my heart was pounding a mile a minute.

The moment was quickly arriving when I would make the deal and my body was shaking from the anticipation because I couldn't believe what I was about to do. Here I was walking around school with a .45 semi-automatic weapon in my backpack and doing all of this to get some baseball cards. The thought of getting caught and what the consequences would be if I got caught had never crossed my mind.

The morning bell rang, and it was *GO* time! I walked inside the classroom and put the backpack right next to me on the ground. I took my seat and waited for class to begin. Julio sat right across from me. I let him know I had the gun and was ready to give it over to him.

I was feeling like I was about to throw up because my nerves were a wreck! I had never felt emotions like this before as my heart was thumping so loud I could feel it inside my ears! I was starting to tremble because this way of making money had brought me to a whole new level. My mind was dialed in and I could feel all of my senses had been heightened as I was constantly looking around the classroom as if anyone was watching me. Time had instantly stopped as I sat there waiting for the deal to be finalized. I was loaded with excitement and anxiousness as I was ready to get the money and get this over with.

We were in the last row inside the classroom so no one could see or hear us. Right there in the middle of a class session, I opened my backpack to show Julio what I had brought, and he instantly liked it, so I pulled the gun out of my backpack and put it inside his.

This whole thing was absolutely insane - we did this right there in the classroom! I mean, talk about doing one of the dumbest things you could ever think of, and it was at the top of the list as one of the all-time dumbest things I could have ever done!

I quickly gave him the gun, he gave me the cash and I put the money inside my backpack, and we were all set. Class had gone on for about an hour but it seemed like the longest hour ever! Now all I wanted was for the day to end so I could head back home and start spending.

As the school day was ending, I decided to skate home instead of heading straight over to the card shop. I wanted to take a little time to think about what I was also going to buy with the money and not be too impulsive, for once.

Chapter Ten

After waiting a few days, I was about to leave the house and go to the card store and buy that cool Ken Griffey Jr. card. After all, this was the reason why I sold the weapon in the first place. As I was about to leave the house with my skateboard, what happened next was like something that came right out of a movie.

Right before my eyes a police car pulled up to the house with an unmarked car. An officer along with another person in plain clothes got out of the car and walked up to my front door. I stood there frozen in my tracks and did not know what to do. I tried collecting my thoughts as my mind was racing a million miles a second. I had a good idea about why the police were at my house, but I didn't want to say anything until I learned what they actually wanted.

The officer rang the doorbell, and I answered the door. I was the only one at home at the time because both of my parents were working, and my brother was still at school. As I answered the door, the plain clothes person didn't waste any time asking me if I had taken a chrome plated gun from his house.

Come to find out, John's dad, Terry, was the person in plain clothes! Unbeknownst to me, John my source for all of the knives and ammo, had all of the weapons and ammo stockpiled inside his house. Nothing was accounted for in any way except the .45 because his dad was using it for his protection piece. After Terry questioned me for a few minutes, all he had mentioned was the .45 because as he stated before, it was the only one he really kept track of and he knew it was missing.

That played out well for me because as far as he knew, I only had one of the guns and nothing else. I tried to change the subject and asked him what he did for a living and he said he was a gun dealer and had been in business for a long time, which explains why he had so many guns and knives lying around the house.

I was instantly cleared of all the other items but was still in a very bad situation; I still was on the hook for the .45 and he wanted it back, like right now. I told him and the officer I did not have it in my possession but a friend of mine was holding on to it for me. BS was flying out of my mouth, and I was saying anything and everything I could to get out of this situation. The officer told me I had until that same night to get the gun back so we could get this all cleared up. I agreed and said I would get the gun back as soon as possible.

As the uniformed officer, plain clothes officer, and Terry headed back to the patrol car, I went into total panic mode because as the officer was walking out of the house my mom was walking up to the front door. I could see my mom walk over to the car and as she did, everyone got back out of their cars so they could explain the situation.

After about a 10-minute conversation with the officer and the plain clothes gentleman, my mom came storming up the walkway and went right passed me and into the living room where I was sitting on the couch. She did not say one word nor did she even look in my direction. She went right to the phone and proceeded to call my father.

Oh Boy, this was it! She explained to him over the phone what had just happened and all I heard was, "I'm leaving work and on my way back home.

"Aw crap! Here we go again!" Another mess and another day of trouble! I looked at my mom and told her that I had to go somewhere and would be right back. She looked right at me and said, "The hell you are!" You better sit your ass back down and wait till your dad gets home!"

I had never seen my mom as angry at any point in my life until now; this was an entirely new side of her, one that I never knew existed. She was so mad all I could see was steam coming out of her ears and her face was red as red can be! I then sat back down on the couch waiting for my dad to come home so I could get the gun back from the kid that I had just sold it to.

As I sat there thinking about what was going to happen, my brother, Jason, strolled up along with his friend, Danny. They walked into the house and saw me sitting on the couch with my hands holding my face up. Danny had seen me sitting and as I tried to get a word out, my mom yelled at him to go home. He looked back at me and immediately bolted out of the house and didn't look back.

Jason asked me what was going on and my mom explained to him what had just happened. He, too, was frozen stiff and said absolutely nothing; actually, he also had a part of getting the gun, but had nothing to do with it after I took ahold of it. He then went into the bedroom and stayed there until our dad got home.

About an hour went by before my dad's car pulled up in front of the house. All I could do was sit there and think about what I was going to say and what I was going to do to rectify this situation. But after all, what could I really say? I was absolutely sunk, drowning with no life raft.

As he parked the car and got out of it, he proceeded to walk toward the door and was getting more and more pissed with every step he took. I mean it looked like he was aging with every step he was taking! As he entered the house, I expected to hear screaming and the fists would be flying but he looked straight at me and asked me what had happened.

I explained what I had done with a gun as I had sold it to a student on campus and now the owner wanted it back. The words "sold a gun" passed right by him because he wanted to get this mess over with. My dad then asked me where the gun was now and I explained to him I had sold it to another kid and that it was no longer in my possession. He asked me for the kid's number, but I told him that I needed to talk to him first. He had this look on his face like, are you kidding me? Why do you want to talk to him first?

He just stood there saying nothing, so I gave in and dialed up his number. He then took the phone out of my hands and talked to Julio for about 15 minutes and explained to him what had happened with the police. My dad told Julio that he wouldn't be in any trouble if the gun was given back to us without any issues. Julio agreed that he would give the gun back and I would give the cash back to him as well. We all agreed to meet in front of the school campus because it was in a public place so there would be nothing to worry about.

An hour went by, and we were about to leave when one of the patrol cars happened to pull up again in front of our house. The officer proceeded to walk up and as my dad answered the door, he asked about the gun. My father explained that he had contacted Julio and we all agreed to get the gun back to the owner. The officer said he was going to join us in case anything went bad. I asked, "What do you mean by that?"

The officer explained that anything bad means Julio may not want to return the gun and decide to do something stupid like get into a shootout or something else along those lines. I was now feeling the tremendous weight that I had caused from all of this. The stress had felt like I was holding a fifty-pound backpack strapped to by backside and it was getting heavier by the minute.

As my father and I got inside the car, it was total silence; neither one of us had anything to say and wanted to get this whole thing behind us as quickly as possible. We drove off with the patrol car following right behind us; we pulled up alongside the campus and got out of the car with the officer. We all stood around waiting for Julio to arrive with the gun. The officer started asking me some questions like, was the kid a gang member? Was he always into guns? Was he ever arrested?

I answered no to all of the questions, and he asked me why someone would want to have a firearm like that anyway. I told him it could be for anything, protection from someone, maybe someone at home, who really knew? I told the officer I had no idea why he would want the gun. All I knew was that he came to me and wanted one, so I got him what he wanted.

After finishing up with the questions, I saw Julio walking up. I told the officer I was going to talk to him first so I could get this handled and once I got the gun back, he was free to walk back the way he came.

The officer agreed and all he wanted was to get the gun back and make sure no one got hurt. When Julio approached us, he had a backpack around his shoulder. He took it off and put the backpack on the ground. The officer asked Julio if the gun was loaded, and he said no and that the magazine was sitting next to the gun.

I looked at Julio and told him that everything was cool, I returned the cash to him and once the officer got the gun, he was good to walk away like nothing had ever happened.

Julio looked at me and asked me if I was all right and I proceeded to tell him that everything was cool. As Julio unzipped the backpack, he slowly put his hand inside the bag and pulled out the gun with his hand on top of the barrel instead of grabbing it by the grip. Julio took it out he handed it straight over the officer along with the magazine.

After the officer looked the gun over and got everything back, he told Julio he was free to go and that no charges were going to be filed against him. Julio then glanced at me and asked if I was going to be all right. I told him I was good for now, shook hands, and off he went. I then asked if I was free to go since John's dad got the gun back and everything was settled from the incident, but as quickly as I asked the question, he looked at me and told me no.

"No? What do you mean no?"

The officer said we had to follow him back over to the owner's house for some more questioning and to see what Terry wanted to do, more specifically if he wanted to press charges. Aw crap! Just when I thought this whole ordeal was finally finished. I could only imagine what was going to happen next. My dad and I got back inside the car and followed the officer back over to Terry's house.

As we pulled up and got out of the car, Terry was waiting inside, speaking to one of the other officers. Another officer walked over to me and wanted to ask me some more questions, such as if was I a gang member, what did I want the firearm for, why did I take it in the first place?

His questions were passing right through my mind, and I couldn't think. Could I tell them I just wanted to buy things I did not really need in the first place. But this had always been about getting an adrenaline fix and this was another opportunity to do so.

The officer went back inside the house to talk to Terry, I instantly had the thought that they weren't going to take me to jail! There's no way I am going to be arrested by some cop! I'm going to run and hide because they're never going to catch me! My dad looked over at me and could tell what I was thinking and told me not to do anything stupid and make it worse.

I just waited for a decision. When the officer came back out he told me to stick around because they were asking the owner what he wanted to do about this situation. Wanting to do what about the situation? The officer told me they were talking about if he wanted to prosecute me for stealing the gun which meant an automatic lockup and a felony record! I stood still and did not say a word.

My dad looked over at me again and said I will always remember this, how the punishment will fit the crime. If the gun owner presses charges and I go to jail, that was my fate and if he doesn't, then I was supposed to learn from my mistakes and chalk this up to another one of life's lessons learned. There was no way I was going to walk away from this situation without something happening and getting arrested, there was no way!

Shortly after my dad finished talking to me, the officer who asked the questions said, "If it were up to me, I would put you in jail with no questions asked." I was so lucky the decision was not up to him! He kept talking and saying the same phrase a few times, but I tuned him out rather quickly because I was more focused on what the owner had to say and not him.

After another fifteen minutes, the patrol officer who originally came with us to get the gun back came outside with Terry. I looked at the both of them, my body shaking and sweat was starting to pour out of my body, while I stood frozen in my tracks. This was it! My time had come, and I was going to get handcuffed, put in the back seat of the patrol car and sent to jail!

Terry looked at me and asked if I learned my lesson? It took me a couple of seconds to answer because of everything that was running through my head. But when I finally could speak, I looked at him and the officer and replied in a low subtle voice, "Yes sir, I totally learned my lesson and it will never happen again!"

Terry then turned to the officer and said there was no trouble with the situation and he was not going to press charges because the gun was given back to him and there was no damage caused by me taking the gun.

Um what? Did I hear him right? I stood in utter shock. I was like, *you're not pressing any charges?* Wow! Terry looked at me and said no, then told me to stay straight and stay out of trouble. I put my hand out to shake his and as he shook back. I had to ask him one final question, why was that his favorite gun?

He replied that it was his protection weapon in case someone broke into his house and wanted to bring harm to him. I told him I understood perfectly and thanked him once again. I quickly started walking back to the car when the officer, the one who wanted to throw the book at me, had crazy look on his face. He was also surprised the owner was not pressing charges and his crazy look was one of, "You lucky little bastard!"

I provoked him a little by smiling back and told him to enjoy the rest of his night! I could not help it because of the way this had unfolded, and I wanted to let him know everything was as it should be. My dad and I got back inside the car and as we were driving off, I looked at the officer again, gave him another smile and waved goodbye as we took off to go back home. He just continued to stare as we drove off and I hoped I would never see his face again.

Our ride back home was a quiet one. I tried not to think about of any of this ordeal and pushed it out of my mind. When we pulled up to the house, all my father said was I am the luckiest person on the planet right now in that I was not going to jail.

He could not believe what had just happened, but more than that, he was shocked that I walked away from it all. He did, however, hold up his side of the punishment: if I was released from this whole crazy ordeal, it would be a life lesson. With all of this happening he had agreed to everything and as we walked through the front door, my brother and mother were sitting on the couch and asked what happened.

He explained what had happened and my mom shook her head as if to say you're a lucky bastard! I told them I was going to bed because I was exhausted, and I was pretty sure everyone else was too. I went to bed and wanted to put everything behind me and move on from this mess.

As I got up the next morning, I was still spinning, imagining how I could have ended up in jail and much worse, been tagged for a felony.

When we got to school, I saw Julio in class and we talked for a bit. He understood what had happened and everything was cool between us because no one went to jail over this. We walked away with no issues.

I also wanted all of the heat to calm down before moving on to my next adventure.

Chapter Eleven

School was getting increasingly tiresome, especially when I was sitting in class all day. To my thinking, the sooner I was out of class, the sooner I had time for more excitement. It got to the point that I didn't even want to study anymore so I decided to skip it all together.

After a while, I really didn't care much about school, seeing no real value in what I was learning. I started to keep my books open while I was taking exams and got busted quite a few times. I mean, when was I ever really going to use any of this stuff? I just wanted to get it all over with and move on.

One particular student I started to get to know was James, who was in the same class and was laughing when I had been busted for cheating. We become really good friends during the school year, which I can also say, carried over with him getting into my shenanigans.

James would come by my house and I would introduce him to all of the different sports and I'd also show him the different types of sports cards you could collect. He was amazed at how many cards I had collected and was curious about the cost because, after all, I wasn't working to pay for them. I told James they didn't cost me any money and I got most of them for *free*. It was after all, for me, more about the excitement in getting the cards and pushing my limits with not getting caught.

Now he wanted to know how I did it because he wanted to get into collecting and accumulate as many as I did. I told him the upcoming weekend he should stay over and we would take a walk to the store and pick some up. I told James to also bring a jacket because he'd need it for the store.

We went inside the store where all the sports cards were displayed and browsed around. A new shipment of hockey cards had come in that day and there were boxes all over the isle. I instructed James to watch me as I started to load up. My heart was starting to pound to the beat of a drum and my body started to shake with excitement as I opened a box! I took about 10 packs and put them inside the sleeves of the jacket. I then turned to James and told him to do the same.

He was amazed at how many packs I had stuffed inside my jacket! There were maybe about 20 packs stuffed inside my sleeves and I told James we should go up to the counter and buy at least a couple of packs so as not to raise any suspicion.

My body was starting to shake more rapidly and I was now starting to sweat a lot more as I walked up to the counter and paid for a couple of the packs. I was trying to calm myself down as I walked out of the store; I didn't want to arouse any suspicion, but it was getting harder by the minute from all the shaking my body was doing. We both left the store without getting caught but, now he was as hooked as I was, wanting to go back and get more and more.

After several trips, he amassed quite a collection. It was so easy for him to get more and more packs and he wanted to ride that train as long as possible.

I knew my time was running out with the possibility of getting caught or for something to go wrong. Every time I went back to the store, my body was shaking less and less. My heartbeat was not so prominent and I was becoming less focused with each trip. With the sense of excitement quickly fading away, this meant the book was about to close and something was about to happen.

On one particular weekend, we both walked up to the store and everything was business as usual. I started to put the cards in my jacket, but this time, I wanted to go out with my biggest stack of packs. When I loaded up and walked up to the counter, I reached into my pocket to take out some cash and while doing so, I felt the entire stack of packs slide my right down my arm to the cuff of my sleeve!

If you were standing next to me, you could see the whole thing from the outside of my jacket and see them slide all the way down on the inside! If I hadn't had a tight cuff on my wrist, the packs would have slid right out and landed right there on the checkout counter!

This time around, my heart started to beat so frantically, I thought it was actually going to pop outside of my chest and run out the front door! I also felt like buckets of water were being poured over my head with how much sweat was coming out! I literally thought I was on the cusp of getting caught!

James stood there and went pale white because he didn't know what to do. He couldn't believe what had just happened and thought I had just been caught red handed. Luckily the cashier didn't see anything and I continued on with my transaction.

I looked back at James and calmly continued about my business as if nothing had happened. I made some small talk with the cashier to distract her while I paid for the packs. I looked back and told James that I would meet him outside. I nonchalantly walked out the front door and kept walking down the street until he caught up with me.

He kept saying how lucky I was and that he couldn't believe I didn't get caught. He seemed very impressed with how calm I was when the packs slid down my jacket sleeve. I told him I couldn't panic because if I did, I would have gotten caught, so I knew I had to keep calm the entire time.

As we were walking back to my house, I was now feeling the effects of what had just happened. I was dripping with sweat and my entire body was shaking with every step I took. I also felt a different sensation, one with almost getting caught. Having experienced that sensation of almost getting caught this had now opened another gateway into my life.

I still didn't know what I liked more, getting all of the packs, or the excitement of almost getting caught? It seems crazy, but I really got a kick out of feeling the excitement and the overwhelming sensation that came along with almost getting caught. My hands were shaking as well as my entire body every time I thought about it! It felt exhilarating and I needed more!

After I eventually calmed myself down, I told James I was done for a while because of the close call, but mostly because I was ready for something better. He wanted to go back for one last score and call it quits.

The next day we headed up to the store, but this time he didn't wear a jacket because we were out during the daytime. Without a jacket, he was left stashing the packs inside the front of his pants. I told James it was not a smart idea because if he wasn't careful, they could fall right through his pants and end up on the floor.

When he was ready, he grabbed a couple of the packs and put them down in the front of his pants…just like I told him not to. You could only imagine what happened next; he overloaded his pants with way too many packs.

Incidentally, there were no cuffs on the bottom of his pants to keep them secure. The packs went straight down his pants and actually landed on the tops of his shoes! I knew exactly where this was going, and I told James he was going to be in trouble if he kept stuffing them down his pants but, of course, he still didn't listen.

James mentioned that he had taken as many packs as he could and we then headed down one of the isles. As he was walking closely behind me, out of nowhere, I saw a pack of cards fly right by me! I looked behind me to see what happened and there he was, standing right in his tracks with the look of a deer in the headlights! I asked him what happened. He said that one of the packs had slid down his pant leg and as he moved his leg forward, the pack flew out of the bottom of his pants and then it was kicked forward by his motion.

Inside I was laughing, but I had to keep it together because he was panicking and telling me the packs were falling down his pants! I couldn't believe what I had just seen! I pulled James over to the side and told him he needed to figure out how to secure the packs or he was going to get busted. He picked them up and kept trying to stuff them back inside his pants like he did at the beginning.

At that point I didn't even pay attention to what he was saying because I got sidetracked and my head was floating. I kept looking around the store as if I wanted to take something as well. At this point, I just heard James keep saying, "Eric they keep falling, damn, there goes another one!"

He started freaking out and picked the same pack up and stuffed it back into his pants, with the same results. I thought I was inside a cartoon because he was doing the same thing over and over again with the same result! You could almost hear the laugh tracks playing in the background during this crazy scene.

When James had snapped me out of my distraction, I told him to take the packs out of his pants and just leave them behind. The last thing he needed was to start walking outside the front door and suddenly have one of the packs fly out from the bottom of his pants. Someone was bound to see it.

Or worse yet, having all of the packs fall out at the same time. His panic mode was still kicking in and I told James to cut his losses and be done with it all. As I left the store, I officially closed the book on taking sports cards.

After seeing what had just happened with James and my close call from earlier, trading cards were no longer giving me the excitement I was looking for.

Now I was on to the new chapter looking for my next adventure.

Chapter Twelve

While I was a Junior in high school, I had brought myself to the brink of another life altering experience. In chemistry class we had been split up into groups of four to work on some new experiments. Out of nowhere, one of the kids in our group reached into his pocket and pulled out a penny. He then asked if we dared him to throw the penny at the front of the classroom, towards the teacher. Two students in our group decided against it and didn't dare him to throw the penny. I, on the other hand, dared him and told him to go for it. "Toss it up and let's see where it lands."

He reached back and tossed the penny towards the teacher. It bounced for a bit and finally landed on her desk. She immediately sprang up from her chair to see what had flown over her head bounced, off the wall and landed on her desk. Everyone was quiet because no one had actually seen anything and were unaware of what was going on.

As she picked the penny up off of her desk, she looked around the classroom and announced, "Whoever threw the penny was lucky I did not see them or they would be going straight to the principal's office for an automatic suspension."

Well, you would think anyone in their right mind would have taken those words to heart and listened, but once she ended her warning an idea sparked in my head. She mentioned it was extremely dangerous for anyone to throw things inside a classroom, especially if they were aiming at her. On the last statement of her reprimand, she stated "What's next, a student in the classroom throwing bullets at me?"

Now again, anyone in their right mind would have taken this warning to heart and would think twice before even thinking about throwing a bullet at a teacher!! When she finished up with her statement, we went back to our experiments, but I was still thinking about how he had gotten away with tossing a penny inside the classroom and no one had said a word. Then I thought what if a bullet was tossed inside the classroom? What would be the real consequences of doing it? How much trouble could I really get into?

As the day ended, I walked home thinking about how I could do something similar. The word bullet kept creeping deeper and deeper into my thoughts. After the whole ordeal with the gun situation from the prior year, I had gotten rid of everything that came from selling the weapons, everything except for one round that I had kept as a reminder. I had put the bullet on top of my dresser; it was just sitting there for the last few months collecting dust.

When I got back home from school, I sat in my room staring at the bullet for about an hour, wondering what I should do with it, while all kinds of ideas were going through my head. I couldn't for the life of me understand why it was still in my room anyway since I should have tossed it out a long time ago. I mean all this stuff ever did was bring me nothing but trouble anyway. I kept telling myself over and over again that I should just throw it in the trash and be done with the whole thing once and for all.

But for the life of me, I couldn't walk away from all of what was going to happen. This prank also had the possibility of being something big, which was something I hadn't had in a long while and this would be a big one at that! Later that night, I went to bed wondering what I was going to do, was I or was I not going to do this?

When I woke up the next morning and got ready for school, I decided right then and there I was going to make a decision. As I was walking out of the house, I grabbed the bullet from my dresser, put it into my pocket and headed to school. I met up with James along the way and was totally silent on the whole situation. I stayed mute regarding what I was about to do.

Chemistry class came around and I was a little bit nervous because this prank could end up in several different ways. It wasn't like the balloons I used in grade school; this was a live round I would be using. I had every opportunity to back out of doing the prank but kept pushing myself forward.

We got into our groups and as we started our experiments, I asked the group if they remembered what the teacher had said when the penny was thrown at her. I wanted to gauge their reactions. They all had replied yes especially the kid who had thrown the penny to begin with. I also asked if they remembered what she said about someone throwing a bullet at her and of course they all said yes. I saw what their reactions were and at that point I reached inside my pocket and pulled out the bullet.

All three in the group sat and stared at me with a look of, *you have to be out of your mind to bring a bullet on campus!* They couldn't believe I was willing to take it this far especially after the short period of time since the penny had been thrown. The kid who had tossed the penny kept asking me if I was actually going to go through with it while the other two kept telling me it would be one of the biggest mistakes I could ever make.

In hindsight, I should have listened to the other two students but, hey, I came this far, right? Why stop now?

As the teacher started her lecture, I had the bullet sitting in my hand, my body shaking with all of the excitement tearing through me! It was as if my insides wanted to scream out from all of the buildup I was feeling! I was back to a state of craziness and chaos and I was loving every minute of it! It was one of the greatest feelings in the world! Having all of my senses waking up at the same time! This prank was bringing me to the top of the mountain!

When she was deep into her lecture, I moved the bullet around and cupped it tightly inside my hand, I was ready to toss it up in front of the class towards the teacher. I kept hearing the conflicting comments from the group with one of them saying go for it, and the other two saying don't do it. I finally made up my mind and put the bullet in my three fingers and was about to toss it up in front of the class. I could feel all of my muscles shaking as my hand was gripping the bullet tighter and tighter!

All logic and sanity were put by way side, my heart was pounding a mile a minute! A part of me didn't want to do it but at the same time I was lost in the moment. I looked up at the teacher to see where she was standing and if she was able to see what I was about to do.

She was off to the side helping another group with their project and she couldn't see where I was sitting. As she was helping that group with their project, I crouched down and tossed the bullet towards the front of the classroom. The bullet was on its way! I had now crossed the point of no return. I remember just sitting and watching the bullet fly through the air and wondered where it was going to land. Instantly I was hoping it would stay out of sight and she wouldn't see it.

Eventually it hit a wall and then bounced off another wall before landing in a matter of mere seconds, I had gone from sitting in a group, to throwing a live projectile at a teacher inside a classroom! What the hell! All of my senses had come crashing down! My heart had come to an instant stand still!

Now the bullet had landed and was only a matter of time before she saw it. I sat in disbelief and was feeling major regret, but it was too late.

After the bullet was tossed, there was nothing I could do. I would have loved to turn the clock back and not throw the bullet at the teacher, but it was too late and the clock was ticking forward.

Our group just sat quietly as could be. No one said a word - what could they really say? The two that said *no* were still in shock and the one who said yes was still smiling. After hearing something bounce around and landing close to her, the teacher was totally startled and wanted to get to the bottom of what had just happened. She started to look around the classroom to see what all the noise was and where it came from. She was frantically searching all over the place for what created the noise because she didn't know what to expect. I mean it wasn't too long ago that someone had just thrown a penny.

She finally found what had caused all the commotion. Now, as I was saying before, I was stupid, stupid, stupid for doing this from the beginning. My concern was where the bullet had landed because it was the last place anyone would have expected. Personally, I think at that point the universe was looking at me saying, "Let the punishment fit the crime for being so stupid."

And it surely did!

She had a briefcase with her lesson plans for the day and had it open on her desk in case she needed something. Well, as she was finishing up her search for what was thrown at her she finally stood up and walked over to her briefcase. She stared inside for a few seconds and her eyes got wider. She then pulled out the bullet and held it straight up in the air!

Was everyone really seeing what I was seeing? Because after throwing the bullet in the air and bouncing off a couple of walls, it had landed smack dab in the center of her briefcase! Of all places, right in the middle of her briefcase! I knew she was going to find out who had thrown it because she instantly yelled out, "Who threw this!" Who was the person so reckless and irresponsible!"

Finally, she said that if the person who threw it would confess to her and they would not be in as much trouble. She would just deal with the students one on one, with no principal involvement.

I should have just spoken up and admitted it was me, but for whatever reason I was thinking I was going to get away with it, like so many times before. I just sat quietly not saying a word. It was also because since no one else was talking and not saying anything, possibly that would be the end of it. Finally, after speaking with the class for several minutes, she went on to say that if no one was willing to step up and admit what they did, she was going to call the principal to clear up the situation. I sat there saying nothing as did the entire class.

She kept saying she wanted to take care of this herself and she was getting a bit more pissed because now she said she feared for her life. I still sat not saying a word because I think at that point I was in total denial since I might still get away with it. With no one in class speaking up, she had no choice but to call the principal down so he could take care of the situation.

We all sat quietly and as she was on the phone, a couple of the students in the group asked why I hadn't said anything yet. I looked at them with a blank look on my face and told them I had no reason why I wasn't talking, but I think it was because I was now shit scared of the consequences! However, I still had the illusion everything was going to work itself out and we were going to move on like nothing ever happened.

When she got off the phone, she notified the class that the principal was on his way down and this was the final chance for the person to turn themself in so things could be worked out with the least amount of damage. Not a word was spoken. I still said nothing. I now had every chance given to me to make all this right and accept the consequences, and I was paralyzed with guilt, but I couldn't admit to being responsible.

It didn't take to long for the principal to get to the classroom and when he walked inside he looked around to see what was going on. He asked the teacher what happened and how bad the situation was. She told him that a student in the classroom had just thrown a bullet at her and she now feared for her life, and she didn't feel safe inside the class. Something had to be done immediately.

Shit! What the hell was I thinking! I bow down to you chaos because you got me once again! The principal asked the classroom if anyone knew who was responsible for throwing the bullet. Again, no one responded. The principal sat there for a couple of minutes looking around, waiting to see if anyone would answer, but still there was silence. There wasn't even a hint about the culprit.

His next strategy was to take out a couple of sheets of paper, fold it over and tear off several small squares. He then told the class there was nothing to be worried about and that they could anonymously write the name of the person they thought was responsible for throwing the bullet at the teacher. He assured the students they would be held harmless and there would be no type of reprisal for naming the person responsible.

I didn't know it at the time, but with all of the *seeming silence* inside the classroom, actually, word was traveling really fast to the name of the guilty party; everyone was starting to whisper to each other saying "that's the guy, it's him over there". In other words, the whispers across the class were of one name and one name only, Eric! Everyone had that piece of paper in front of them; they were free to write anyone's name!

I looked around and saw each small square with my name scribbled on it. It was only a matter of time before my name was called out and my fate was officially sealed. There was absolutely nothing I could do at this point. There was no telling what was going to happen because of all of the whispering and seeing my name written on all of the squares around me. I left my piece of paper blank because I mean really, what was the point in filling it out?

The principal walked around the classroom and picked up everyone's square, it was pretty much over for me; I was figuring everyone had written my name and I was done. He came to me and asked me to turn mine in; I reached out and gave him a blank piece of paper and didn't even look at him. I just put it in his hand and he looked at the next student as he walked past me.

It was only a matter of time before my name would be called out! He came down to the last couple of students, took their papers and then proceeded to walk out of the classroom and headed back to his office so he could identify the person. He told the teacher he would be back shortly to let her know who the person was and finally take care of the situation.

Reluctantly the teacher went to teaching the lesson for about 15 minutes as we all waited for the principal to return. She was still a bit nervous, apparently wondering if something more could still happen. The waiting time seemed eternal. Every minute that went by was another minute waiting in anticipation; what was going to happen to me? How far was the punishment going to go?

After about twenty minutes, he finally returned. He whispered to her the full name of the student and then at that very instant, be blurted out, "Will Eric Trapasso please stand up and follow me to the office."

As soon as he called out my name, I had about a thousand different scenarios running through my brain. I was totally busted and there was no way I was going to get out of this. I then got up out of my seat and as I started to walk out the door with the principal, I could hear all of the whispering going on. I didn't take anything with me; I just left everything sitting on my desk.

By this time, I was filled with guilt and anxiety. I went from feeling like I was standing on top of mount Everest, to one of my biggest regrets and bewilderment. I was trembling from all the anxiety, waiting to hear what he was going to say. It literally was one of the longest walks I had ever taken in my life; it was like time had slowed to a standstill.

My thoughts were still racing with visions of the kind of punishment I was going to suffer from this, but now the thought of what my dad was going to do to me was creeping into my mind! I didn't even think of him at first because I thought this would have turned out a very different way with a different outcome. I was given every chance to fess up, but I was too chicken shit to say a word.

As we turned the last corner, he escorted me into his office and told me to take a seat. He also let me know someone was waiting for me but before he brought him in, he wanted to get my side of the story.

Oh crap! Was that my dad waiting out there! Was he already here? I then thought to myself, "Wait a minute, there was no way he could have gotten here this fast from work and for one brief second, I was thankful it wasn't him! I knew eventually I would be feeling his wrath but not just yet. I was momentarily spared a few seconds from his punishment.

In the meantime, I was talking to the principal and explaining to him what I had done and gave him every detail about how I thought throwing a bullet in class as a joke. I told him that I finally realized that I had misjudged my actions and made a poor decision. I really hadn't thought of the psychological damage my action could cause.

My teacher was now going to forever remember a moment in her life when someone had just done something stupid to her. Shit! All she was doing was trying to teach students so they can better themselves and I briefly took that away from her. Now she will always have this imprint in her mind, an imprint that took away her sense of safety.

As I was explaining all of this to the principal, it was finally sinking in that my actions had serious consequences. He sat silently listening, just looking me in the eye, letting me talk through my explanation. I could only imagine what was going through his mind as I was speaking. I bet at that point he wanted to strangle me; to be honest I couldn't blame him if he did, and I would have done the same thing if our positions were reversed.

Finishing up with my side of the story, he sat back and finally started to speak. I remember him saying what I did was one of the most stupid things that could have ever happened and there were going to be some really serious consequences. He went on to say he was now going to bring in the person who was waiting for me outside his office. He got up, opened the door, and called him in. My eyes were wide open waiting to see who it was.

After about ten seconds, a uniformed police officer walked into the office and stood staring at me! I couldn't believe it!! An Anaheim police officer was called in to see what the incident was about because he had got a call about an explosive device being tossed inside a classroom!

Explosive device! Holy crap! I was so rattled I was sweating like I had just run a five-mile race, and I was trembling beyond belief. As he walked into the office and sat down, the principal gave the officer a brief explanation about what had happened. Right off the bat the officer stared at me and gave me a dirty look while listening intently to the principal.

After I explained my side of the story, the principal relayed the teacher's side of the story. After he explained everything, he wanted to know from the officer's point of view what kind of consequences were going to come from this. The first thing the officer said was the teacher could press charges for assault with a deadly weapon!

I screamed out, "Assault with a deadly weapon, are you kidding me? How could that be assault with a deadly weapon? "The officer then looked at me and said the bullet was a live explosive and it could have gone off if it were to land on something with the right precision and strike point. His reasoning was even though there was no real weapon to fire the round the bullet, it is still considered a weapon and could go off and kill someone.

I thought to myself, “That’s it, I’m done!!” I sat totally shocked since I couldn't believe what he had just said. Right after the officer gave the principal his reasoning, he said he needed to go back to the classroom and ask if the teacher was going to press charges for assault. The principal then proceeded to get up out of his chair and told me to go wait out in the hallway.

I then got up and walked out into the hallway as he walked back to the classroom.

As I walked out to the hallway, the officer was right behind me. I remained silent. I was worried that if I said anything, he could use those words against me. He then broke the silence and spoke out by explaining to me that what I had done was really stupid. More so it was borderline psychopathic because when I gave my side of the story, I was calling what I had done a prank, not realizing I was putting someone's else's life in the balance. He also proceeded to explain to me over and over again the bullet could have gone off at any time when I threw it at the teacher.

All that for what?

Well, in my stupid way of thinking as a young punk teenager, I questioned the officer right back. I asked how a round could fire off if it were not loaded inside a gun? How can it explode and kill someone with only having the slimmest of margin of something coming into contact with the firing pin? I stood there with a smirk on my face as if I were the expert on everything and was like, *take that copper! Think you’re so smart, do ya?*

He then looked at me and laughed and said all it needed was the smallest type of pinpoint like landing on the corner of a desk or anything which was sharp that would allow the bullet to fire off and do harm to someone.

I was still questioning him because in my mind, it still didn’t make a lot of sense. But, after all, he had the upper hand and said, "It doesn't matter what we both think at this point because if the teacher decides to press charges, you are going straight to jail"

Damn! He was right, there was no fighting or arguing at that point. He then said I was really lucky it didn't go off and kill someone, if it did, I would be going to prison for murder, instead of a lock up for assault. I finally decided the smartest thing for me to do was just shut up, just shut up and stop talking because all it was doing was pissing the officer off and I was not helping the situation in any way. In fact, I should have listened to myself earlier and not said a word.

I just looked at the officer, closed my mouth and looked away.

After about ten minutes of waiting, the principal finally returned and told us to go back inside the office because he made a decision. To be honest, I was scared shitless; I didn't know what to expect because this was going one of two ways. I was going to jail or I was going to be suspended. The principal then talked to the both of us and explained that the teacher was not going to press any charges because the bullet didn't hit her and no one was hurt by my actions. I held my breath as he was giving us the decision.

When he finished, I finally exhaled, but it didn’t really feel like a sigh of relief. I felt like my head was going to explode or I was going to pass out because of all of the anxiety and anticipation.

While the principal was still talking to me, he looked over at the officer and let him know he was no longer needed and he was free to go. As we all stood up, I looked at the officer and you could tell he was aching to take me in and make an example of me. He looked at me with a stern look on his face, put out his hand and said, "You were very lucky today that your actions didn't cost someone their life".

I then put my hand out to shake his. This felt like Deja vu all over again! My memories form what had happened with the guns not too long ago came bubbling up. This was lucky strike number two with law enforcement and once again I narrowly escaped being arrested.

When the officer left, the principal told me to take a seat because he was now going to explain what was going to happen next. “Oh boy!” He repeated what the officer had just said that I was very lucky with this whole situation and thankfully no one was hurt, or worse, killed. With that said, he was now on to the matter of my consequences.

He explained first and foremost, I was on an automatic suspension of five days and I was not allowed on or anywhere near the campus. While I was on suspension for the five days, he was going to notify the school board and request that another thirty days suspension be tacked on, which at that time was the maximum time allowed for a student to be suspended from school. He actually preferred to go to the school board to have me expelled from the entire district. Even though I had gotten off from the charges, he was going to push for the maximum penalty he could give a student. I was not entitled to be on the campus anymore because of the great harm I had brought down on one of his teachers and he said he would see this through until I was kicked out of his school and prevented from enrolling in any other school in the district. Even though I had escaped the major penalties, he wanted to bring the house down on me.

All I could do was sit there and just listen and not say a word as he was handing down the maximum punishment. But, of course, his words were going inside one ear and out the other because all I kept hearing was expulsion. I just waited for him to stop speaking and wait for the next thing to happen so I could get this over with.

As he finished up, he said I was done for the day and now free to go. He repeated that I was no longer allowed on school grounds for at least the next five days. He was also going to notify my parents about what was going to happen with me on the thirty-day suspension and how I was going to go in front of the school board with the expulsion.

I then got up from his desk, looked him in the eye, said thank you and walked out of his office; I didn't want to make matters worse.

As I started to walk out of the office, I heard him pick up the phone and start dialing. I knew he was now calling my parents' house to let them know I was being suspended.

I started my long walk back home and was doing some major reflecting. I felt like I was in a crazy dream and couldn't get out of it. I was going to wake up at any moment from this crazy nightmare! But this was as real as it was ever going to get. I already knew there wasn't much I could say to my parents since I was caught and identified by other students, when they had anonymously written my name down on paper. I started to think more about my future. If I were to be kicked out of school, were would I go? Was I allowed onto another campus, or would they kick me out as well? The questions were endless. and I walked as slowly as I possibly could. What was the rush to get back home? What was waiting for me?

I took every twist and turn I could find. I might have raced a snail if I could have found one. Eventually I made it home. I didn't know it at the time but my mom was home early because she had taken a half day off.

When I walked up and opened the door my heart started to pound, as if it were going to rip outside of my chest. This was crazy fear and major anxiety stuff! I walked in and saw my mom sitting in the living room on the couch. I looked over and was hoping she had not heard the phone message.

Maybe I was lucky at least for the time being. But what I didn't know was she was in the kitchen at the time and actually heard the entire message! I tried to play off being home early by telling her it was an early day at school. It didn't fly. She looked back at me and said she heard the whole message and my dad was on his way home from work.

All I could say was, "Aw crap!

She then replied, "Yep, aw crap is right!"

I went to my room and sat waiting, waiting for him to come home, and having to explain why I was suspended from school and finding out what was going to happen to me next.

After an hour or so of waiting I heard the car pull up and heard my dad's footsteps walking up the walkway. By that time, I decided to go into the living room and wait for him to come in. This way I would already be in there and see how pissed he really was. I then saw his face and it had the same look of death on it. He flung the door open, walked inside and asked what had happened; I didn't say a word.

I let my mom explain what she had heard on the answering machine. She told him to listen to the message because it was going to explain everything. He walked into the kitchen and pressed the play button. I swear you could have heard a sizzling noise coming off of him because he was so pissed. It was like the sound you hear when you cook beacon.

When the message ended, he turned to me and said I was grounded till hell freezes over, and that *heaven help me* if I was expelled from school! That was it, that was pretty much all he said. I thought there would be more but he was so pissed he couldn't stay at the house. He then walked outside, got back into his car, and headed back to work. I looked at my mom to see if she was going to add anything and all she said was for me to go back to my room and stay there.

I got up and headed straight back to my room while keeping my mouth shut.

I knew the next several days were going to be very intense because no matter what I did around the house, it wasn't going to matter because I was on suspension. More importantly, I was on the brink of being expelled from school. For the time being, I was getting my homework from each of the classes from my brother.

By this time my dad had had enough of me getting into trouble and I was not allowed to communicate with anyone until this was all over with.

Here we go again…

Chapter Thirteen

All I had was time…I tried to do as much homework as I possibly could to keep time moving. My five days flew by, and I was now entering day thirty of my suspension. It got to the point where I thought of giving up on all of my homework because if I was going to be kicked out of school, why do it anyway? But I did the bare minimum just to pass the time. My routine was *to do homework, watch TV, do homework watch TV*. Everything else was off limits.

After a few weeks, I was finally asked to attend the school hearing. This was going to be the DECISION Day. Was I going to be expelled or allowed back on the campus? It would take all my energy to prepare my defense, plead my case, and explain why I deserved to stay.

The hearing day arrived, and I was as prepared as I was ever going to be. When we arrived at the school, I started off on the wrong foot, because I actually came to campus in sports attire instead of following the guidelines stated in the hearing notice – dress appropriately. Personally, I didn't care what I looked like. I figured why would it matter anyway? Boom, instant bad impression because of my perceived attitude.

As I walked into the conference room, I could hear the whispers and see everyone pointing at me and saying, “That's the guy. He's the one that threw the bullet at the teacher!” None of their opinions mattered to me. I knew no matter what I said, absolutely nothing would change their minds.

I sat down and assessed the room. There were district school board members, about five witnesses from my class, and I guessed there were notes from the teacher. The panel had decided that since all of this started on the Loara school campus, it should also end there too. If their decision ended in my favor, I would be told I could go right back to class since we were meeting on campus. The examination was under way as each of us started to explain our own versions of the incident, including explanations and opinions from the witnesses in the class.

I was shaking with anxiety and sweating through my clothes as everyone was talking.

The principal relayed the information from the teacher, how a student (me) had brought a bullet to a classroom and decided to throw it at the teacher as a type of joke, with no regard to the other students or any thought of the possible consequences. This continued with each one of the witnesses as they described the same scenario over and over again for the next couple of hours.

Each one of the students who were in my went on to explain how I took out the bullet out of my pocket, sat it down on the table and said, “I was going to throw this at the teacher!” One of the students went on and said, “I told him not to throw it but he would not listen to me” While each witness had a somewhat different twist, it was all the same stories.

All of them ended with each stating, “I heard something hit the wall and land in a briefcase” The teacher testified last and she went on to say, "I felt like my life was being threatened and something needed to be done." But I believe the most damming part came when she said, "I gave the person who threw the bullet every opportunity to come forward but they never did. I wanted to have this taken care of internally but when that person never answered, I need to take this matter to a higher level." I knew from her saying that I was given every opportunity to answer and I never did, showed everyone at the hearing I didn't care what was happening and I took everyone's safety away.

After all of the witness testimony was completed, it was now finally my turn. I literally opened up and spilled my guts saying, "This was all supposed to be a harmless joke and no one was going to get hurt." I even went on to say, "I didn't ever think that the bullet was ever going to go off which is why I tossed it in front of the classroom to begin with." leave out any detail no matter how small. I repeated over and over again to the school board saying, "What I had done was supposed to be a total joke, a very twisted and demented joke, but merely a joke and nothing more." I wanted them to see that by me saying "Joke" over and over again, something would be changed in their minds. Which would eventually lead them to believe that it was a harmless joke and nothing more. Every phrase had the words, "Bad joke" in it which I was hoping would persuade the board to give me just the suspension.

At this point, I was feeling guilty about what I did to the teacher. I went on to say to the board, "I am totally responsible for all my actions. I had played a really bad prank on a teacher who did not deserve that kind of attention at all." The guilt was starting to at me up on the inside and I was feeling the crushing blow from everyone's testimony. I looked around at everyone's facial expressions and all I would see is utter hate and how they despised me. Personally, I couldn't blame anyone else for my actions nor could I.

As I continued my story, I told the school board where I had gotten the idea how a student a couple of weeks prior to my incident had thrown a penny in front of the classroom and got away with it. That is what had given me the idea of throwing a bullet at the teacher because she had explained to the class the student had thrown a penny at her and was worried someone was going to start throwing bullets.

She also said she was fearful, which meant she was no longer going to put up with anyone's nonsense.

Finishing up my final testimony, I deviated way off into something different. For some reason, I had come to the conclusion that with everything I had testified on was going to get me off the hook. More so, I didn't believe that I was going to get any more of a serious sentence. I guess maybe it may have even been the sense of excitement of sitting up on the stands looking out at everyone, but the sense of guilt had worn off.

My mind had totally shifted in a different direction in believing I could now say anything I wanted to without any consequence. My body was starting to shake with excitement with the ideas turning in my head. More so, I was the center of attention, even though it was negative attention, It was attention none the less. I thought to myself, "I can say anything I wanted to, no matter how outlandish it was!" I was having all of the same symptoms whenever I was going to have a rush with rapid heartbeat, eyes dilating, sweating, body shaking and a sense of euphoria.

I don't know why or where my next explanation came from, but I had to be one of the stupidest comments I could have given at the end of my testimony! I couldn't believe I was saying this, but I said, "I was always playing with live bullets, throwing them against walls and fences to try and get them to go off and actually fire!" I even said, "I wanted to see what kind of damage a live round could make when it went off."

What the hell was I thinking in telling them that! Stupid! Stupid! Stupid!! I couldn't shut myself up as the words kept flying out of my mouth! It was one hell of an adrenaline rush that I was having but one that had put me over the top in looking like a total

Sociopath or even a Psychopath! Or maybe even both mixed together!

Not surprisingly, the school board was in total shock as they stared at me probably wondering if I had totally lost my damn mind! Or were they listening to some type of unstable teenager.

Honestly, I couldn't blame them after those stories; if it was the other way around, I would have thought the same thing. I was such an overconfident dumbass because of the constant desire to be above everyone else. That, along with the constant desire to push boundaries had made it even worse!

I had actually said that I was always throwing the bullets against the walls and fences to make them go off. Who does that? I pretty much just buried myself with my own testimony. Overall, it was sounding like it was an open and shut case because here was a student that willingly wanted to strike out against a teacher by throwing a bullet at her, but at the same time, a student was also throwing the same type of bullets at walls and fences to get them to fire. It seemed like every time I opened my mouth to say something, I was digging myself a hole and burying myself deeper in my own grave.

Even with what I had said, I was delusional enough to still believe I was going to be cleared of the charges.

After finishing my side of the story, the board had heard enough. One of the board members asked me if I had anything else to say. There was one thing he was looking for, one simple phrase, "*I AM SORRY.*"

Everything else spilled out, but that phrase never came out of my mouth. I had given up everything I could about what I had done, holding nothing back, but I still left out the most important words. One of the school board members made a comment and to this day what he had said makes me think about what a stupid decision I made.

That school board member asked me point blank "Do you have any regrets?" He warned me that my reckless behavior could possibly affect my life for the foreseeable future. Moreover, if I had the ability to take back what I did, would I? I couldn't get any words out; I didn't have the guts to pony up to the wrongdoing and take responsibility for my actions. In my mind, it still was a prank that went wrong. Good old narcissism!

Everyone waited for my response and for me to show remorse. I still sat motionless and couldn't muster up the words to speak. Maybe it was fright or more likely in my mind it was too late. My head was spinning.

After what felt like forever, I could sense that everyone on the panel felt that all of their questions had been answered. It was obvious they had all made their decision. The school board president announced that they had listened to all of the facts and opinions from the teacher and witnesses. They heard my personal testimony to defend my action. After counting the votes, they had all come to the conclusion that it was best for the teacher and the school as a whole that I, Eric Trapasso, was to be expelled immediately form Loara High as well as from the entire school district.

As our meeting concluded, I didn't know what to say or how to react, since I was in total shock and my head was still spinning. I was one of the last to leave the conference room because I was still soaking in one hell of a reality check. The principal stayed behind so he could explain to us what the next steps were going to be.

I was ordered to leave the district once my suspension was finished. That was it, plain and simple. I was to be expelled and given a written notice of my expulsion so I could take it with me when I applied for enrollment at another school. Still in shock over the decision, I really thought I was going to be just suspended and afterwards allowed back to school.

I looked over at my parents' faces and their expressions said everything. My dad had a scowl on his face, which showed utter disappointment in my actions and my mom just looked down into her hands, just so she didn't have to look in my direction. They both in essence had different ways of showing their disappointment. Not a word was said by either of them once the decision was rendered.

I could feel my self-destruction with every minute that went by. There was no discussion when we left the campus and headed back home. At this point, what else could really be said? Absolute silence, not a word was said. I was done and my goose was cooked.

After we got back home, we went inside the house and my dad actually left and went back to work. I knew he didn't want to be near me, so it was just my mom and me until my brother got home, and it was just silence for the rest of the day.

Chapter Fourteen

A crazy idea surfaced, I felt I needed to apologize to my chemistry teacher. I was finished there anyway, but I wanted to let her know how sorry I was for dragging her through this mess. Since both my parents were about to leave for work, I figured I could sneak out for a little bit and head over to Loara.

When my parents left, I got changed and headed out. I still might have a little time to talk to a couple of the teachers who had really helped me out while I was in school. I went to my psychology teacher first because he was a great person and was one of the coolest teachers. He thought I was done with my suspension, and I was back in class and didn't think anything of it. I sat and listened to him go on like always about the psychological views of people and why they did things in their life that were good and bad.

He always taught a great class because of how much detail he went into.

As he finished and class was getting out, I asked him what he had heard about my situation. He said everyone in school had heard about me throwing a bullet at a teacher and he was actually surprised I was let back into school. He was curious as to why I did it. I admitted I made a bad judgement call. I also explained if I could take it all back, I would rewind the clock and would never have done it.

He explained if I ever needed to talk to him in confidence or ever needed some therapy, he would be there to help me out. I looked at him shook his hand and said thanks and that I would always remember his words as I go forward in life.

Now on to my chemistry teacher who suffered the most from my supposed *prank*. I had major butterflies in my stomach because I was going to see her for the first time since the review board. I didn't know what to say to her and I wondered if she would even want to see or talk to me. With the little bit of time I had left, I ran over to the classroom to where it all started. I walked inside as class was getting out and most of the kids had gone.

As I worked my way up to the front of her podium, she glanced over to my direction and saw me standing there. I was frozen in my tracks and shaking all over because I still didn't know what her reaction was going to be. Finally, as she made eye contact with me, the other kids still in the class recognized me and were now all silent. I walked up to her and finally got my words out. I'm not going to lie; I was very scared and nervous coming back to class.

I started to speak and as I got my words out, I felt myself tearing up, I was actually tearing up! I felt myself going into a total guilt sensation with the feeling of remorse weighing me down. It felt like I was wearing a one-hundred-pound bag of weights on my back. My very first word I finally got out to say was, "Sorry, I am so sorry for my actions."

What happened next was a total shock to me. She actually looked back at me and gave me a big smile! Holy crap! A smile! Did she really do that? She then asked me how I was doing, and the conversation changed from my regret and remorse to her understanding and forgiveness.

I told her I was hanging in there and getting by day by day and explained my expulsion. I then shifted the conversation back to her and asked her how she was doing because I wanted to deflect all of the attention from me back to her.

Quickly her mood changed to sadness, but it had nothing to do with us. She had turned the conversation on to her son and explained how he was always into drugs and could never get himself straightened out no matter what she tried to do for him. She also tried to get him into rehab, but it didn't work either. I asked her what his name was and when she responded, I immediately had a major flash back and instantly remembered who he was!

I remembered it so well because one day a guy named Richard came over to the house when everyone was out. He had asked if I wanted to hang out for a couple of hours because he had to go over to someone's house to pick some things up. I said why not since I was sitting around the house anyway.

So, we headed over to his friend's house to pick some stuff up. He knocked on the door and a young guy answered. Richard started talking about buying some stuff from him, so he pulled out some money and the guy who answered the door gave Richard his items. While we were all standing in front of the house chatting, he rolled up some of the stuff he had just purchased and we all started to smoke it.

I introduced myself to Richards's friend. He appeared to be about eighteen and seemed to be high. He had asked if I went to Loara and I let him know I did something really stupid at school and was currently suspended. I didn't give him the details except I had really messed up and was just biding my time until I got the official word for the expulsion.

We continued to talk for a while and as we were still smoking, I asked him how he and Richard knew each other. I remembered the guy saying both of them would do all kinds of drugs all the time and it didn't matter what it was, especially the harder the better. He also went on to say how he had worked that entire summer and made a few thousand dollars but instead of putting any of it away, he and Richard used it all up on drugs, every last cent of his paycheck!

All that money wasted on drugs, with nothing to show for it! But he said they had a great time getting high as a kite. Richards friend was standing rubbing his hands on his face as he was also in total disbelief that he worked all of that time and had nothing to show for it except for getting high all of the time with Richard. Overall, you could tell he didn't really care that he wasted all his money. Richard didn't seem to mind either and was more concerned about getting his fix.

We talked for a little bit longer and as we finished up, I gave Richards's friend a handshake and told him it was good meeting him. He told me that if I ever wanted anything from him no matter what it was to get high, that I knew where to find him. I said thanks and we went our ways. That was the one and only time I would see him ever again.

The teacher went on about her son, saying he was always getting himself into trouble and couldn't seem to stay out of it, especially when it came to drugs. She looked over at me several times talking about her son in a very "past tense" sort of way and she wished there was more she could have done for him but couldn't.

Right then and there I knew where this was going; I just continued to let her talk and did not say a word. As if I couldn't get any lower, she dropped the heaviest bomb of all by saying her son had just recently committed suicide because he couldn't cope with life anymore. The drugs had taken a heavy toll on him. I had no idea this had just happened; it was right in the middle of my suspension when he had decided to take his own life.

She looked directly at me and explained her son was not happy and had not been happy for the longest time. She had suspected he was doing drugs because of his personality changes, but more so because he was as high as a kite when she came home, and he never had any money. Every time she asked him and called him out if he was doing drugs, he always told her *no* and lied right to her face.

She went on to say one afternoon he got so depressed he decided to end it all. He walked over to an overpass on top of a freeway then jumped off, killing himself instantly. He was only seventeen at the time, seventeen! Not only did I put this woman through hell by throwing a bullet in class, but now she had to deal with her son killing himself weeks.

I had to look away from her several times because when she was talking, I had to hold back my own tears. It was hard because I had recently seen Richard and if I knew, I would have told him his mom was one of the greatest teachers who had ever taught at Loara High School. No, not a word was said by me because I didn't know who he was; I didn't know he was the son of a great teacher who had put up with a lot from one particular student.

I could have said anything to him to see how he was doing or if he ever felt like dying, but I didn’t. I just listened to him telling stories of getting high over the summer.

When she stopped speaking, I could see in her eyes that she was also holding back the tears, she wanted to let them out because of all of the hurt she was feeling. Instantly I went right over to her, grabbed her, and squeezed her with such a big hug. I didn't want to let her go because I really felt good doing it and I didn't care if anyone saw it. I mean, really, what was anyone going to say about me hugging a teacher? I was already expelled anyway, and they couldn’t do anything else to me.

Here I was, showing empathy for someone hurting- a totally new experience for me. And yes, my tears were falling; this whole story was so emotionally overwhelming. As I let her go, I brushed my face and rubbed my eyes. She looked at me and said, “I know you have been through a lot yourself but no matter how bad things get in life, it never gets that low to where you feel you need to end it.”

Also, she told me that if I ever needed to talk to someone when things got really bad in life, she would be around for me to talk to, but especially if I ever had any thoughts of suicide, she would be there for me and I should call her immediately. She couldn't stress that enough and repeated it several times because she not only wanted me to hear it but everyone else who was still inside the classroom.

I told her I would call her, but thoughts of suicide had never crossed my mind; I had enjoyed life too much to go down that road. I mean, I wanted to feel alive every single day. I gave her one more hug and said I had accepted the consequences for what I had done, and I was going to be expelled once my suspension was up. I told her I took full responsibility for my actions and then I asked her for her forgiveness. She looked at me and replied that she had forgiven me a long time ago and had no ill will towards me.

I looked at her and once again I grabbed her and gave her a hug, I could see her eyes tearing up as she could also see mine with every hug. I thanked her one last time and walked out of the classroom never seeing her again, hoping for the best for her.

That day would be the end of me stepping onto Loara High School grounds as a student. I said my goodbyes to the few the teachers and students I wanted to see. I walked off the campus still feeling those mixed emotions I still had to deal with the next couple of weeks of the suspension and not to mention what was going to happen after I got expelled. I walked back home to an empty house and did some homework.

I had paid another steep price for giving into my desires of excitement.

Chapter Fifteen

By now, I was just buying time until school let out as my parents were still deciding what they were going to do with me. I needed to get back into school and at this point, any school would do. I felt like the best thing I could do was go away for a little while until things cooled down. James and I talked for several days and came up with a game plan.

We would ask our parents if I could stay at his house for a couple of months. I was still grounded, but I felt like I needed to get out and do something because all I was seeing were these same walls over and over again. Surprisingly, my parents were good letting me stay over there for the summer, but they told me I needed a game plan to give to them so they would know what was going on and what to expect.

After a couple of days my dad called over to James's house and talked to his dad, Jeff. He went over his agenda. I was to be solely at his house for the summer and I was not allowed to come back home for any reason except when the summer was over. Once I left home, I would be their responsibility.

I was I totally blown away that this was actually happening. I was excited because I felt like I had to get away from the world and get away from all of the trouble or the possibility of trouble. After everything was set up, I packed a small bag and grabbed what little cash I had at the time.

I called James to let him know I was all packed up and ready to go, so he walked over to the house, sat outside, and waited for me to come out. I told my parents I would use this time to sort things out and get better control of myself.

When we were walking back to his house, I had so many ideas that my head was spinning. The thought of what I was going to do with my life repeatedly came to mind. Everyone else around me had some sort of direction, all except me. I was always more interested in making money than going to school, especially if I didn't have to work to earn it. Something had to go one way or the other because I needed to get my diploma and choose some sort of career path.

I walked inside and told his parents they rocked for what they were doing for me, and I would be forever grateful. James's mom, Elaine, was really cool; she always gave us our space to do what we wanted to do as long as we stayed out of trouble. She and I had a brief conversation. She wanted to know what had happened to get me into this situation. I first asked her what James had told her. and as it turned out, it was very little.

So, I explained everything, and I mean everything, from the beginning to the end, which was my expulsion from school. She was supportive and from that point on never brought it up again. She actually told me that I was welcome over at any time.

After we finished talking, I went into James's room and put my stuff on the bottom bunk while his younger brother, Nick, crashed out on the couch. One aspect of pushing my boundaries was that it had led me to develop an addictive behavior. This had led me to try alcohol for the first time, and knowing that I had an addictive personality, drinking would temporally fit the behavior.

On one particular night, when James's family left for the night, I went into the fridge to see what was in there. In the back there were a couple of beers. I was curious to see what all the fuss was about with drinking. I reached inside the fridge and took a bottle. I popped the top and took a drink! As I was drinking the beer, I had a disgusted look on my face.

The beer was nasty stuff; I couldn't believe people actually drank this! But even with the bad taste, I still drank it! I drank it slowly because I didn't know how it was going to affect me.

By the time I finished the drink, I could feel the buzz. I was smiling for no reason, then it went on to giggling at the dumbest little things, like when a commercial came on, I thought it was some of the funniest sayings I had ever heard before. By now I knew the buzz was in full effect and I had hit the peak. My head was spinning, but I was having a great time. Especially for having my very first beer. The night went on and the buzz was starting to wear off; I was finally getting tired and decided to crash out for the night.

When I woke up the next morning, I didn't have a hangover, considering I only had one drink. It was something I wanted to try again next weekend, since his parents were out for the night and the house was empty. I knew this would be the start of adding another addiction, but at that point in time, I didn't care about the consequences.

All I cared about in that moment was feeling good! To be able to not worry about any type of consequence or for that matter, let go of all the stupid things I had done in the past, is what mattered more to me.

As the week went on, I talked about getting a couple of his dad's beers and saving them for Friday night. So, what James and I did was go into the fridge and take out a bottle from the pack in order build a small stockpile. This way his dad would think that he was drinking them every day, but in reality, he would have one less without knowing it. It worked out perfectly! His dad never noticed.

Overall, this was very cheap stuff, which probably accounted for the disgusting taste. For giggles I asked his dad what it cost when he bought one of the twelve packs. I remember him saying he was getting a twelve pack for something like around four dollars. Now I knew why the stuff tasted so bad!

When the weekend rolled around and everyone headed out for the night, we went out to the garage and cracked open a few of the bottles. This time the buzz was kicking in even more because instead of having one, I drank two of them relatively quickly.

Out of the blue I had a notion of wanting to cook up some food. The next thing I knew was we started to grab everything and anything that was not nailed down and we were either grilling, frying, or baking it! I dove into the fridge and started to make burgers, hotdogs, and anything else I could cook.

While all of the cooking was going on, I grabbed a couple more beers and drank them one after another. By this time, I think I was hitting my peak with a buzz. The night was going great and getting better and better because of the food, beers, and music! I didn't want it to stop because it was one of those moments that made you feel like nothing else mattered.

By now my buzz was getting stronger, which meant the music was getting louder and the room was spinning around more and more. I cracked open another drink with dinner and was now going for it all. After we were done stuffing our faces, we looked around the table and saw all of the remaining food sitting still waiting to be eaten. I had filled myself to the brim and was getting overloaded.

I had also come to the conclusion that we had prepared way too much food because of all the drinking.

After finishing up, since we couldn't move anymore, we packed all the food back into the fridge, saving it for the next couple of days. There were still a couple of drinks left, but we decided to save them for the next time. I was feeling the height of the buzz and I knew what was coming the next morning, something that everyone who over drinks and regrets having to experience…the hangover.

Morning came rather quickly, considering I went to bed so late and had several drinks. I had my first official hangover on record. Surprisingly, it didn't come off as severe as I thought it was going to be, for the time being anyway. I guess with all of the food soaking up the alcohol, it didn't hit me as bad as I thought it would.

My brother, Jason, was starting to call over because he was bored and wanted to hang out with us. He was calling all the time for us to come over to the house and play baseball like we always did on the weekends so many times before.

When we finished up playing baseball, we headed back to James's house. My brother wanted to hang out with us, so he decided to walk back to the house with us. As soon as we got back, we wanted to go to the garage and turn the radio on. But when we walked into the house we saw his parents sitting in the kitchen apparently waiting for us.

I thought they were going to say something to us about all of the food we had made the previous night. His mom mentioned there were lots of leftovers sitting in the fridge and she wanted to know where it all came from. James and I explained we had made some things last night because we wanted to stay in and cook instead of going out, but since we made so much food, we decided to put the leftovers in the fridge for the next couple of days.

To our surprise she didn't have a problem with any of it because after all, nothing was wasted and there was still plenty left over for everyone to eat. The only rule she had was from now on we were not supposed to make everything in the house at one time. I told her it was no problem and that was the end of that discussion. We were still a bit surprised because we thought they were going to be really pissed at what we had cooked and how much we had made.

But in the end, they weren't very upset at all. After everything was all cleared up, we went back out to the garage and turned the music on. While Jason was over, we noticed the dart board hanging up in the garage. We decided to have some fun while trying to sneak in a beer whenever possible. I picked up the darts and started to throw them, aiming for certain numbers and colors. As soon as the first dart hit the board, his dad heard the darts and immediately ran out to see who was throwing them. This is when the fun began!

Both James and his dad let the trash talking come out and it was a constant barrage of insults. Jeff would shout out, “He couldn't hit the broad side of a barn!" James laughed back and said, "Ok old man, we’ll see who has more game!"

From then on, they challenged each other while Jason and I watched them play a round to get used to the game. It was funny in the sense that while each one of them took a turn at throwing the darts, the other one would start talking all kinds of trash on the other person. I would sneak off to the side while they were playing and grab a drink, trying to down it as quickly as possible. I didn’t want to make it too obvious, so I kept it at two drinks and was feeling the buzz!

Then I’d start to laugh at the stupidest things while they were playing, but I had to keep it under control to not make it so obvious in front of his dad. They both continued to play and the score was close until Jeff threw the last dart and beat James at the game. It was great because when Jeff beat James the trash talking continued and went on for hours, neither one of them letting up.

Jason and I were laughing our butts off because this was the first time either one of us had ever seen anything like this before. I couldn’t stop laughing because I was feeling the buzz from the beers. James could tell that I was acting weird, but he couldn’t put his finger on why.

After they finished the game, James’s younger brother Nick came out; he had heard all of the talking going on during the game and he wanted in on the fun. We decided to play teams because my brother and I now wanted to join in on the game.

It started off with James and me against Jeff and Nick. When I was ready, James asked if I had had a couple of drinks. He said he could smell the beer! I gave him a shush laugh and was ready to go. I picked up the darts and threw my first one at the board and it stuck in one of the numbers we needed. I wanted to continue playing, except now I wanted to play with a beer in my hand instead of sneaking it off to the side.

Ever since I threw my first dart all I wanted to do was play the game all night long with everyone. It was a lot of fun. It wasn't like selling a gun, throwing a bullet at a teacher, or doing something else along those lines, but for the first time in a in a long time, I was having a good time and I didn't need to go after that adrenaline rush that I was always craving. It was a great feeling to be able to be myself and I didn't have to worry about doing anything crazy or stupid.

It was keeping me out of trouble for the time being. I liked every minute of it. Darts were a good outlet for me because of how they took my focus away from doing stupid things. Even though I wasn’t old enough to drink, I considered having a few beers a lot safer compared to doing all that stupid crap from before.

I couldn’t hit anything on the board because I was feeling a buzz and couldn't help but laugh at every throw. Sometimes I just tried to hit the board and not anyone else around me. It was a lot of fun and after playing for a couple of hours Jeff decided he was done and went back into the house.

Once Jeff went back inside the house, I wanted to bring some drinks out. I already had a couple and wanted a few more. So, I went to our secret stash and took out a couple more beers. When I picked up the darts and was ready to play, I cracked a beer open, and chugged it down as fast as possible.

As I think back on it, drinking and playing darts wasn't one of the smartest things to do because I was still learning the game and the beer kind of distorted reality. I was spinning from the drinks which didn’t make it any better.

With the four of us playing darts and having more drinks, time was flying by. This time though, I did not have all of the food inside my stomach, absorbing all of the alcohol. I was starting to feel the buzz a lot more and things were spinning more quickly than I had ever experienced. I was laughing at the dumbest things again just like before.

Jason decided that it was getting late, and he was going to head back home. Nick also called it a night and headed back into the house. James and I continued to play and had some more drinks until we finished the last few we had stashed away. Finally, around midnight, I decided to call it quits. I, as casually as possible, crawled into the bottom bunk, crashing out instantly. I just knew I was in for a more severe hangover...

The next morning when I woke up, I felt what an actual hangover was like and having a severe headache at the same time. It was hard for me to get up, but after about an hour, I finally crawled out of bed and had to shake things off. It was important to act like nothing happened because I couldn't let anyone know we had been drinking last night. I talked to James. and we got a game plan together to keep ourselves as far away from his parents as possible so they couldn't smell the beer on us.

After I showered and changed, I headed into the living room and tried to keep my distance. If one thing can make a hangover even worse, was music! Sure, enough, as soon as I sat down, the Beatles came on and it sounded like a loud piercing fingernail being scratched on a chalkboard! I was dying sitting in the living room; every song that came on felt like someone was kicking me on the side of my head! I could only stand about 15 minutes of misery before I decided to go back into the room and sleep things off for a while.

I crashed until the next morning. I chalked the previous night up as a learning experience and one I promised myself (with my fingers crossed) I would never repeat. I even went so far as to say that I was never going to drink again, (with my fingers crossed) much like I told myself hundreds of times later on in life, but that never happened.

It's funny because life has a way of giving you different perspectives. One day you might say to yourself, "I'm never going to do that again," but never stick to it. Feeling bored, I called my brother Jason to see what he was doing, and if our parents were out of the house. He mentioned they wouldn't be back until later on in the evening so we would have some time to hangout before they got back home.

The first thing I did was look to see if there was anything to drink around the house. My parents were not drinkers but had a cabinet that had some alcohol in it. There were some old champagne bottles along with some other bottles, so I decided to take out the champagne and chill it in the fridge.

While the drinks were chilling, I went over to my dad's stereo and cranked up the music.

My adrenaline was starting to kick up because my parents were not home, and I was about to drink again! I finally popped the champagne bottle and started to down the bottle.

James, Myself and Nick

I knew I was going to hear it from my parents when they saw a bottle was missing from the cabinet, but it was even more exciting and important for me, taking a big risk and living in the moment. Now feeling the buzz from the champagne, I needed more! Just knowing that my parents could have walked in at any time and got caught, made my heartbeat even faster!

Nothing else mattered except alcohol had taken over my emotions and thoughts. All I wanted was that moment in time, pushing the boundaries as far as I could possibly push them, knowing that I could have been caught at any moment. That was the trick though, pushing just far enough to see what I could get away with and how long I could keep it keep it up for.

After a while, I knew I had to get back to James's house, so I cleaned up and as I was leaving, I grabbed the empty bottles to take them out to the dumpster. It felt like forever walking back to James's house. I made it back and was still feeling buzzed from the champagne and I wanted to keep it going with more drinks.

I asked James if there was anything left in the house to drink, and he remembered there were a couple of beers sitting out in the garage. I pounded a few more down and let the rest of the night play itself out. Eventually, I could feel myself winding down form the drink and the adrenaline was starting to dissipate. Sometime in the early morning, I crawled into bed and tried to sleep off another hangover.

While I was trying to sleep, my mind started to wander. All I could think about on the positive side was how much fun this was! But, along with the positive was the negative, in that I was still kicked out of school. But I was having such a great time with this moment in life I didn't even think about what was going to happen tomorrow.

Slowly, though, reality was setting in with school starting back up and that I was not going to be there for the next year. James was moving on to the next grade and I was sitting idle. Eventually I knew I had to head back home. Summer was ending and we all had to move forward.

Before I left, I sat and talked to Jeff and Elaine and thanked them for letting spend the summer in their home. I told them I had a great time and I would be forever grateful for what they had done for me.

I knew I had to start thinking about how my addictive personality was destroying my life. If I didn't start to get some sort of control, things were going to get a lot worse…

Chapter Sixteen

I already paid the price for getting expelled; I mean I was stuck at the house with nowhere to go and no direction ahead of me. Step by step, it seemed like I was never going to get back, I was nervous, scared, and anxious, a complete bundle of nerves.

Right before I approached my house, I had to get my thoughts together and figure out my game plan. I opened the door and walked past the hallway; my parents were waiting for me in the living room. My dad asked me if I was ready to get back into the flow of things. I sat down and replied that after thinking over the summer, I was ready to get back into school and get my life back on track.

What I didn't know at the time was while I was staying at James's house, my parents were pursuing several ideas about my future school enrollment. At this point, I was open to any suggestions. So, my dad asked me if I was willing to go to *another state* to continue my education!

My head was spinning again with all of the new opportunities, but the one thing that would be holding me back was that everyone I knew would be left behind. As a teenager, nothing else mattered more than close friends and relationships. For my own piece of mind, I wanted to be certain I had tried everything I could do to stay in California.

So, over the next couple of weeks, my dad made several calls to the schools in the district and asked if there was any possibility for me to enroll, but he was coming up against some roadblocks.

Something I didn't know at the time was since Loara High School was in the Anaheim Union High School District, all of the campuses had access to my records. Every time he made a call to one of the schools, he explained my situation and that I regretted my actions. But it didn't matter one bit.

All they saw on paper was a teenager who threw a bullet at a teacher and had been expelled. That was it - case closed. No one was going to look at my potential enrollment as a new beginning or a second chance for a student had so much remorse.

My dad continued making more calls over the next few weeks, but one by one each potential school fell like dominos. The answer was a resounding NO from every principal. Now the possibility of moving out of state seemed more of a foregone conclusion.

Eventually, we sat down again and discussed all of my options, which were very limited, and we finally agreed that my schooling was now going to take place in another state. My dad then proceeded to call around districts in states like Arizona and Utah. It even came down to where we would even travel out to New Mexico just to see if it would be a possibility.

He was putting a plan together; he was building an itinerary on where we were going to drive, where we were going to stay, and where our stops would be. It seemed like we were going on a vacation with a specific agenda, but in reality, the trip was absolutely not a vacation at all. A decision was made, and we all decided to see if the other states would offer a fresh new start.

That night I went to bed wondering about my future.

Our first stop was Utah. We arrived fairly late and checked in to our hotel for the night. Once the early morning came around, we drove around the city to a couple of the school districts. But as quickly as we had arrived, none of us were feeling the energy in wanting to move to Utah. Every school we had checked did not want to look past my expulsion and their decisions were final. Let's just say that Utah was really quick stop over and we moved on to New Mexico.

We stayed for a couple days and visited some of the schools, but with the same result; none of them were willing to allow me into any of their districts. Another quick visit with no luck. We went back to the hotel, packed everything back up, and were on the road again heading out to the final state, which was Arizona.

As we were getting close to the border of Arizona, I was hoping for the best-case scenario since this was our last and final state! Something positive had to come of this trip! After checking into our hotel, my dad did some calling around and after a few calls, there was some really good news! The principal was willing to talk and see what exactly had happened. We quickly headed over to the school and after waiting for several minutes, we went into his office and had a brief conversation.

My dad began by saying he had spoken to some of the other principals in the area and explained what I had done at Loara, with the prank and how it had cost me an expulsion. He let him know everything right out of the gate, every detail; this way there was no surprises.

When he finished explaining everything, the principal asked me about my grades during my junior year. I told him I had only completed about a quarter of the year and once I was put on suspension, I was not able to complete any of the other courses. He then asked me about the possibility of repeating my junior year because of all of the class time I had missed.

I asked him why and he explained that I had not completed enough credits and if I was willing to repeat my junior year, he was willing to accept me into the school and I would be able to graduate.

Wow! I was seriously getting overwhelmed about the fact I was actually considering repeating the year! This was actually about to happen! After thinking about it for a few minutes, I quickly got my words out and told him I was willing to do it and make a fresh start out here in Arizona.

He then told us he was willing to overlook the expulsion and we could all move forward! But as soon as we agreed with our game plan, he made one final comment. Now it was up to the school board for final approval because of the expulsion. As we left his office, I still had very high hopes and continued optimism for the remainder of our stay.

Shortly after getting back to our hotel, we all wanted to call it a day and just hang out by the pool. I was still excited about the new possibility and my heart was racing with all of the good news. With a new beginning, I was also thinking since I was now going on seventeen, I should be able to get my driver's license! After all, the city was so spread out. I was going to need to drive to wherever I needed to get to! But very quickly, my mind turned to everything stupid I have ever done... ya, there was no way I was going to get my driver's license.

Especially, since my dad had already refused to allow it. I couldn't blame him! After all, I was already doing enough stupid crap and didn't need anything else on top of it.

Our day was winding down and we decided to go back to the hotel room. I remembered I had left my Walkman in the car, and I told my dad I needed to get it out of the car. He gave me the car key and when I got down to the car, I got my Walkman and sat in the front seat.

It felt really cool sitting in the driver seat and pretending to drive. I turned the radio on for a few minutes just to make it feel a bit more real. *Wow!,* I thought, this is what it feels like to drive a car. After a couple of minutes, I shut the radio off and was getting out of the car but before I did, I wanted to have a quick look around. I looked through all of the compartments and couldn't believe I had found a spare key…

"Uh oh!" I thought, I just found a nice shiny extra key.

Now ordinarily, I would have left it alone, and not think twice about it. But, as soon as I saw the key, my heart started to pound! My eyes became dilated as I could now see more sharply! … Just the idea of being able to drive the car! Yes! I grabbed the extra key and took it back to the room with me. I gave the car key back to my dad and told him I was going to crash out. I put the extra car key under my pillow and had ideas turning over in my head for the rest of the night.

When we all got up in the morning, we ate breakfast and my parents decided to go over to the lakeside and hang out for a while. I intentionally lagged behind and said I would be down a little bit. This was the perfect time to go for a quick joyride!

I went down to the car and as I sat inside, weighing out all of the consequences and my options from good to bad. Here I was without a license and had zero driving experience, but once I put the key inside the ignition and instantly I could feel my body tense up! My heart was racing, blood surging through my hands as I was gripping the steering wheel tighter and tighter!

That was it! I was now about to do something insane and stupid!

I put my foot on the brake, shifted the gear in reverse and backed the car out of the parking spot. I pulled out and put the car in drive and I was now driving! I was in total excitement mode! I couldn't believe I was driving around the parking lot in the car, my dad's car! Just knowing I could get caught at any moment made the drive even more exciting! I circled the parking lot a couple of times to get used to how the car felt and see how everything worked. The windows were rolled down and I had the music blasting.

After about five circles in the parking lot, I went back and parked the car back in the same spot and turned off the car as if nothing had ever happened. My heart was still pounding, and my hands were still gripping the steering wheel as tightly as possible. I loved every second of this feeling! I sat there for a couple of seconds taking everything in and enjoying the moment.

Eventually I locked up the car and headed over to the lake. I met up with my family as if nothing had happened, but my body was shaking and I had to sit down quickly before I passed out. My little brother was down by the water, so I decided to go down there with him putting a distance between me and my parents.

After a few hours down by the lake, we called it a day and headed back up to the hotel room. We all got changed, ate dinner, and hung out in the room for the rest of the night. My wheels were turning as I was trying to sleep. Tomorrow was the last day before we headed back to California. I needed some more driving time before we left; I needed to get away from my parents a couple more times before the trip ended.

As everyone got ready for the day, I put the key in my shorts for safe keeping. We headed downstairs to the hotel for breakfast. As we were eating, my wheels were spinning with various plans for the day. I had to find a way to do more driving. We finished up breakfast and my parents wanted to go back down to the lake, which was perfect because now I had an opportunity to drive.

My parents gathered what they needed, and we all headed out. We found a nice spot on the shoreline and settled down. I kept squeezing the key in my hand and was ready for some driving! Once we had everything on the shoreline, my parents headed down to the water and I let them know I was going for a walk to do some sightseeing.

Actually, this was my perfect driving opportunity!

I hustled over to the car, unlocked the door, sat down inside and was ready to go! I turned the car on, rolled down the windows and blasted the radio as loud as it could. I put the car in drive and off I went! My heart was pumping out of my chest and I could feel my body trembling with excitement!

It made me want to test the limits of how fast I could drive the car. I wanted to kick up my driving a bit more and decided to go out on to the major streets. Knowing I had to be extra careful because, not only was I secretly driving my dad's car, but I was also driving without a license!

After about 30 minutes of driving, I decided I should get back to the hotel, especially since I was already pushing my luck. I headed back to the hotel and needed to meet back up with my parents, but I did a couple more laps around the hotel before putting the car back into the
parking space.

Once I got the car back into the spot, I sat there for a couple of minutes, grinning ear to ear. That was some of the best fun that I had in a while and of course, I needed to keep it in control because I needed to come down off the excitement quickly. I didn't want to get back to the lake and have my parents see me all jacked up with a stupid grin on my face. I calmed down for a little bit and finally got out of the car, locked it up and headed back to the lake.

When I got to the shoreline, I found the spot where we were and noticed my parents were still down in the water. I decided to lie out in the sun until they got back, closed my eyes, and relaxed while still trying to calm myself down.

But, since this was our last day, I wanted to take one more drive before we left in the morning.

My younger brother Jamie at 2 years old

Not long after I sat down my dad walked over to ask where I had gone, and I let him know I did some sightseeing around the lake. It was pretty much a check in, just to make sure I was not getting into any trouble.

I figured I would keep it quiet and just let it go, since I wasn't going to tell him, *ya I took your car and drove it around the hotel and the city*! My mom came over and they both said they had enough for the afternoon. We gathered everything and walked back to the room.

That evening we headed out looking for a restaurant and chatted about my thoughts on coming to Arizona. Our conversations were all positive and I was looking forward to the fresh start. After getting to the restaurant, we ate, talked some more, and wanted to call it a day since we were leaving early in the morning.

As we got back to the hotel, I was thinking of a way I could get out and go for one more drive before our trip was over, but I had to come up with something believable. I told my dad that I had left one of my tapes in the car and wanted to go down and get it. He gave me the car key and I bolted down to the car with the extra key in my pocket.

I started walking towards the car and I could feel my heart pounding! All of my senses were starting to become more sensitive! I unlocked the car, sat down, and was preparing for one more drive. This time was different,, being it was nighttime and it was a lot harder to see. I had the windows down, my mix tape in, and the volume way up! I wanted to drive a little farther instead of just around the hotel. I headed out of the parking lot and was heading down the street.

Unaware of my surroundings because of the music playing and how I was bumping along to the song, I made a right turn after the hotel, and I didn't notice I was going onto a major lane with a freeway sign above it.

As cars sped past me, I noticed I was the only one driving slowly and watched them pass me by. It finally dawned on me I was now driving on the freeway! I had hit panic mode because as I was driving, I could see I was passing the hotel on my right side and it was getting smaller and smaller as I looked into the side mirror. I finally hit the "OH CRAP!" button and had to figure out a way to get off the freeway. I shook off my anxiety quickly; panicking was not going to get me anywhere.

After shaking my head, I had to focus on getting back to the hotel. I drove about a mile until I hit the first exit and was doing the speed limit so as not to bring any unwanted attention. As I exited, I saw signs directing me back to the hotel and once I knew I was going in the right direction, happy mode kicked in.

I got the calmness back and got my head together. I followed the signs to get back to the hotel and drove as carefully as I possibly could. I was able to get back to the hotel and felt relieved! As I was driving up, I circled around the hotel a couple of times so I could calm myself down. Feeling more relaxed, I headed back to the parking space, but…there was a car parked right in the space where I was supposed to be parked!

How was I going to explain this one? All I could do was park the car a few spaces over and shut everything down. I sat for a couple of minutes to gather my thoughts, so I could come up with my story.

As I got out of the car, I grabbed my mix tape and headed up to the room. My story was about how a truck was parked so close that you couldn't even open the door and I had to move the car a couple of spaces over so I could get in the car and get my mix tape. After a couple minutes of pleading my case, my mom had asked me if the car was hit or if there was any damage. I told her it was ok and there wasn't anything wrong with it. My dad then looked over at me and asked me if that's why I had taken so long. I told him it was, and I gave the keys back to him and it was the end of the conversation.

I stood there sweating bullets and realized since everything was ok and no damage was done, everything was good to go. I had dodged another fiasco and realized that yes, things could have ended up much worse, but they didn't. I got past that thought and I sat up for a while thinking about the last couple of days of driving.

I had pushed my luck as far as I could take it and needed to put myself in check. I got ready for bed and crashed out thinking about the fun time driving and about the new opportunities that were ahead once I was back in school.

It felt like the night flew by in a matter of minutes because I had my music on for the whole night and had so many thoughts running through my head. I didn't get much sleep at all. I don't know if it was the anxiousness or the mere fact we were going to be heading back home and the fun times were about to end.

With our breakfast conversation focused on all of the changes we had planned, it seemed like everything was going to turn out for the best. For once in my life, I actually felt like I was going to get my act together. It was a good time to talk about how I would be making big changes ahead and how they would shape up in the future. Both of my parents asked me a couple of times if this was what I was looking for and if I was ready to take a leap of change.

After we finished up breakfast, my dad paid the bill and then headed back to the hotel room to finish packing. Within an hour, we were ready for the long drive back to California.

When we started our drive back, I looked out the window at the surrounding mountains, put on my headphones, took a deep breath, and hit the play button. I knew it was going to be a long drive back and I was still doing a lot of thinking. I knew once we were home, my life had to change for the better. I still had to wait for the principal's decision regarding whether he was going to let me into their district. If not, I was going to have to find another way of finishing my education.

But once we were on the freeway and I had my music on the world had seemed as if it had changed completely for the better. At that point in time with the music playing and the window down, I felt like I was on top of the world and I never wanted that feeling to end. I even thought my dad was driving a bit slower too because you could tell he was also in no rush to get back home.

Chapter Seventeen

Exhausted from the long drive, we pulled up to the front of the house. My parents checked in with Jason on what he had done while we were out of state. After they all talked for a little bit, I headed to my bedroom and wanted to rest from the long drive. I crashed out as soon as I hit the mattress and was waiting for the night to end. Tomorrow will be a new day.

My parents left for work and Jason left for school. Now that I was out of school and in a holding pattern, my parents had decided I was going to be a built - in babysitter and they would pay me to take care of little brother, Jamie.

It was an easy gig. I was supposed to pick him up after school and watch him until they both got home from work. After he was dropped off at school, I had the rest of the afternoon to do what I wanted until I had to pick him up. With that much time on my hands, I decided I needed to get out because all I was doing was staying in the house all day. There was a park right across the street and I played some one on one basketball for a couple of hours, until I had to leave and go pick Jamie up.

I met up with James by the baseball fields. We started to talk about how things went while I was on my trip and from there on, the conversation shifted to how I had learned how to drive while I was out in Arizona.

It was really funny how I went on to explain getting the extra key for the car and pretending to be walking around when I was actually out driving my dad's car. I was pretending that I was hanging out somewhere else when in fact I actually wasn't; I was off taking his car around the city for a leisurely drive. I also explained how one night I was driving and ended up on the freeway and it scared the hell out of me! But most of all, my dad had no idea I was driving the car around the city! But I could sense he didn't believe me. I thought the best way to convince him was to take the car out for a joyride.

As soon as I mentioned joy ride, that's when things got serious, and I knew right then and there that we were going for a ride. Our conversation now turned into a "I double dare you" to get your dad's car. I called his dare and told him with a bit of sarcasm, "I will be by at seven o clock and make sure my woman is all dressed up for me," like he was my date. He laughed and said it would be no problem and he would be totally surprised if I was to show up in my dad's car.

Right after I got off the phone, I went inside a liquor cabinet and grabbed some champagne. I popped the cork and took some deep swigs but couldn't get too hammered. After a few more swigs of the bottle, I headed out to go get Jamie. My walk was a very interesting one. I was feeling the drink and was now laughing at things inside my head. The entire walk felt like it took forever because of the slow walking and constant laughing.

When I arrived at Jamie's school, I tried to play as cool as I possibly could without letting on so that I had a couple drinks. I stayed as far back as possible from the teacher so she wouldn't smell the drink on me; I saw Jamie and signed him out. I actually held it together very well! We took our time getting back home; there was no rush after all, as there was no one home and I didn't want anyone to know I had some drinks if they happened to be home.

After about an hour walk, we arrived back home, but I was still feeling the effects of the champagne. Food was my immediate thought. I needed it to absorb some of the alcohol and to take some of the buzz off for the time being. Once I had a quick snack, my mind shifted back to how I was going to pull off getting the car out for a ride. Ah! I came up with the perfect plan!

We had train sets out in the garage and figured I was going to look for some items to build some trains. While I was out in the garage, I could take the car! I still had the spare key. It was fool proof! A quick joyride, put the car back in the garage, close everything up, and go back into the house. It was perfect! Nothing could go wrong with my plan! Just like so many of my plans in the past…

I kept telling myself it was going to totally work out and this was going to be a fun night. After a couple of hours of thinking and waiting for my parents, I knew I had to settle myself down. Around six o clock, my dad arrived back home and walked into the house. I was calm at that point and was sitting on the couch with Jamie watching T.V.

My mom got back shortly after my dad did and now everyone was sitting in the living room watching T.V. Around 6:45 I hopped up from the couch, went into my room to change, and then proceeded to tell my dad I needed to go out to the garage and look for some things out there. I told him I needed to get his keys for the garage, and he told me to grab them from his desk.

As I grabbed the garage keys and walked out the front door, my body was tingling with excitement! I could feel the blood flowing throughout my body with every heartbeat in my chest! I dashed as fast as I could over to the other garage, flung the garage door open and stood there behind the car just staring at it for a couple of seconds.

Every time I felt my heart pound, it was pushing that sensation straight through my body! Once my senses reached their peak, I was dialed in and ready to go no matter the consequences. I put the key in, started the car, and was now on my way up to James's house to pick him up.

As I pulled up to James's house, he ran up and saw me in my dad's car. He was in total disbelief. I was waiting for him to get in so we could go for a ride. His brother Nick also heard the honk and came out to see what was going on and asked where I got the car since he had never seen it before. I told him it was my dad's car and that James and I were going to go for a ride.

He shouted back, "Your dad's car? How did you pull that off?" I told him it was taken care of and we needed to head out since it was getting late.

Once inside the car, we headed off and it didn't matter where we drove, since this was just a joyride with no agenda. I drove all around the Disney area and pulled over to chat with anyone we knew. We circled around several times and after about an hour of driving, I figured I needed to get the car back to the garage.

On the way to dropping James's back home, I gave him the explanation on how I was able to get the car out for tonight and how my plan was full proof and my dad would never know I had taken his car out.

Finally, we made it back and as I dropped James off, Nick came out of the house and walked over towards us. He came over and asked, "Did your dad know you had his car out tonight?" Sensing something was off, I thought, "Why would he know I was driving his car?" I then asked Nick how did my dad knew his car was gone? He then said my dad had called over to their house to see if I was there and if I had seen his car!

Oh shit! My dad knew I had his car!?!? I looked back at James and instantly both of our faces had turned pale white! I was starting to hit the, "OH CRAP!" panic button, since this was all still registering in my head that my dad called looking for his car!

I looked back at Nick and asked what he said. Nick replied that he had told my dad that I was over at their house with his car and I had picked up James to go out for a ride.

Aww crap!! I couldn't believe what I was hearing! I yelled at Nick, “You told him I had his car and I was out with James! Why would you tell him something like that!”

He said my dad already knew I had his car and was over here at James’s house and he had called just to confirm everything. Well, that feeling of adrenaline I had a little bit ago was now drained as fast as I took it in. I was in sheer panic mode once again and was trying to gather my thoughts. I looked at James and asked him if he could come back with me because I may need a fallback story in case something happened.

He said, “Hell no. There was no way I am going near your dad!”

He looked more terrified than I was and there was no way he would come back to my house. Honestly, I couldn’t blame him. If it were the other way around, I would probably do the same thing. I gathered my thoughts and headed out, telling them this may be the last time I might ever see them again!

During my terrifying ride back home, I was trying to put off the inevitable. I was going to be grounded for the rest of my life. Here I was driving my dad's car, without him knowing about it, and I actually thought that I was going to get away with it! After all, I had a FOOL PROOF PLAN!! I really thought I had an airtight alibi from the start, but even to this day, I don't know what made him check the other garage for his car. I was, after all, someone who did not even have a license and didn’t have any type of driving experience. Personally, I just left it as a father’s intuition, knowing something was off and KNOWING ME!

After prolonging the inevitable, I finally reached the end of my journey and ended up sitting in front of the garage for a couple of minutes contemplating what to do next. For whatever reason, I decided to put the car back in the garage the way I had found it. My reasoning was strange because here I was already busted for taking his car out on a joyride. I should have just rolled up in front of the house, parked the car and given him back his keys.

Well, as with everything else bad happening that night, I was now about to drop a nuke on the situation and make it all so much worse.

My mind was all over the place and without knowing it, I had sped up. Instead of taking my time putting the car back, I cut the angle too close from the rear passenger door to the entrance of the garage, and instantly heard one of the most god-awful crunches I had never heard before!

Oh God, now what's happening! I parked the car and got out to see what I had just done. As I walked over to the rear door, I stood there in shear panic shaking from all of the different thoughts and emotions…Was he going to call the cops? I did steal his car after all.

I was sweating bullets and shaking because my anxiety was through the roof! I tried to think, but shear panic set in and my mind had shut down. I couldn't believe I had gotten the right passenger door stuck smack up against the opening of the garage.

What had I done???

It was bad enough that I took the car for a joy ride, now I put a big ol' dent in the door! At that point I didn't know what to do; I mean what could I really do? The car was sticking halfway outside the garage! I was trying to pick up the back of the car so I could move it off of the wall!

I knew my only option was to bite the bullet and get the car off the wall, which meant I had to either put the car in reverse or put it in forward. Either way, the door was going to be a wreck. I got back inside and decided to put the car in drive and once the car moved forward, the only sound I could hear was the aluminum of the door being scrunched inward by the side of the garage. I didn't want to see the damage, but knew I had to see how bad it was. I took a quick glance. I saw the door all pushed in and stood for a few seconds thinking.

I eventually snapped out of it and I automatically went into total depression mode. I walked out of the garage, closed the door, and locked it up. I figured if I told him up front it might make things easier for me because I was headed for a big-time punishment.

My dad immediately bolted towards me and all I could feel was my dad's hands on my chest slamming me against the wall. I didn't have a moment to catch my breath because as soon as he had me up against the wall, the first thing he said was, "Have you lost your mind! What the hell were you thinking taking my car outside and driving it around!" I didn't say a word because really, what could I say? I had bitten myself in the ass once again! I decided the best course of action for me was not to say anything, just keep my mouth shut. He asked me why I had taken his car out and I told him all I wanted was a little bit of fun.

He then looked at me and said, "There better not be any damage to the car or that was going to be it". I don't know if was either sheer panic or maybe even the guilt I was feeling but, I looked at him and told him, "Well there is something you should know. The back passenger door has a small ding in it."

I knew he was going to find out one way or another and I figured this might take a bit of the edge off when he went to inspect the car. He then asked where I got the key, so I spilled the beans and told him I got the key from the small compartment by the steering wheel.

He then looked at me and told me to wait in the living room while he went out to the garage to see how severely damaged the door was. I went to the living room and sat down on the couch. My brother Jason and my mom were sitting there not saying a word and not even looking in my direction.

In the meantime, all I did was sit on the couch and look at the clock while the seconds ticked away. We sat in total silence. You could hear a pin drop because no one was saying a word. Every passing minute seemed to get longer and longer. I seriously thought I had fully driven him over the edge and he would be like, that's it! I'm done!

But after a short while he walked back inside the house and to my surprise, he didn't shout or even get upset, he looked at me and just said, “Get up and go to your room. I will come up there and talk to you about this situation later”.

Woah! He snapped! There was no way he could stay that calm! That’s all he said, just told me to go to my room and wait till he came in there. I quickly got up from the couch and hurried off to my room. I went in and sat at the desk, grabbed my Walkman, put the headphones on and waited. I put my head down on the desk and started to think about all of the crazy crap I have done throughout my short time on this planet.

After about halfway through a song, my dad came into the bedroom. The first thing he said to me was since I was seventeen years old and I was too old to be grounded, that wasn't going to be an option. My punishment mostly consisted of using all of the money I had earned over the summer babysitting Jamie to pay for the damage to the car. In essence, four months of babysitting money was gone!

Since no one was hurt and nothing else was damaged, that made it a bit easier. He then looked at me and asked if I was willing to change my behavior, which would consist of changing the way I loved having excitement in my life.

“Sure, I thought!” But…I didn’t know if I really wanted to change my behaviors at that point…I told him the punishment was fair especially with paying for the damages to the car and in not doing stupid crap anymore…

Around 7 p.m. we were all at the table eating when the conversation started to steer towards what was going to happen next since all of our future plans had been tossed out the window. But just as we started eating, the attention turned to my brother. What was he going to do now that we were not going to be moving.?

My dad was pushing Jason to go into the Navy, but my brother needed to be pushed. So, my dad gave Jason a deadline. He had to have a plan for his life after high school graduation. Jason was not taking any of this seriously and I actually wanted to shout

out, “Dude he's not playing around. He's totally serious and wants you to get on with some kind of career.”

I was always getting into trouble because of my constant need for excitement. I never had to be pushed to make my own decisions, even when most of the time they were bad decisions. Every choice I made took me in a different direction and far off the beaten path. Look at where I was currently, kicked out of school, sitting around, and waiting with nothing to do. I felt like I needed to change my identity to something different, just to get an idea of where I was headed.

This was also when I had adopted a more of a rebellious persona.

So, I decided to adopt a throwback look to the fifties, because to me, it was the rebellious era with James Dean along with Marlon Brando and others. Since I had a lot of time on my hands, I was constantly watching movies from that time period, especially ones with James Dean. He was always rebelling and getting himself into trouble. I watched all his movies and really liked his, “Rebel Without a Cause” persona and the way he dressed the part. Now I also wanted to adopt the fifties look with the hair and the leather jackets; I mean I was even putting Vaseline in my hair! I really liked the rebel look and felt it gave me a better vibe. Now I was dressing the part as a troublemaker because that is what a lot of others saw me as anyway. But I also think I found my new identity. I didn’t know who I was at the time because I couldn’t put myself on a straight path.

It was really hard for me to settle into a routine because I was always looking for the next moment of excitement. I figured I would try something new, wondering if it was going to make any type of difference in my life. But was I going to want to change for the better, or keep making bad decisions?

As we were all finishing up with dinner, the conversation with my brother was basically over and it shifted back to me. Right on cue, my dad slowly looked away from Jason and turned his head in my direction and started to speak to me. He then said, "What am I going to do with you?" I had a hard time mustering any words, but I finally said I was willing to do whatever had to be done in order to graduate.

He then replied, "I will take a look around the area and see if I can find a school that you might be able to attend where you could earn your GED." Surprisingly, the conversation with me was short and sweet because from that point on there wasn't much to really discuss anymore.

Myself, Jamie, and Jason

Chapter Eighteen

After what felt like an eternity, I had finally received the decision from the Arizona school district. I had built myself since we left Arizona in hopes of being able to get enrolled in their school district. I kept telling myself that I had a slim chance, be it a very slim chance of getting accepted but I still kept my hopes up and tried to stay positive.

The phone rang and as my dad answered it, I peeked into the kitchen just so I could listen in to the conversation. He began to talk with the person on the other end and I listened intently, all the while telling myself that everything was going to work itself out! This was going to work! It had too! I kept my fingers crossed and I didn't realize it at the time but I was bouncing up and down because my heart was beating a mile a minute from all of the anticipation!

I stood in my spot during the call, bouncing up and down, with my fingers, toes and even my arms all twisted, just to muster up as much luck as I could. I was even starting to shake because my heart was beating so fast and all of my muscles were really tensed up, I felt like I was going to pass out!

In what seemed like the longest phone call ever, the conversation ended with my dad saying "Thank you" to the other person on the phone. I could see the disgust and disappointment on my dad's face, it was as if he was done with this whole situation. I couldn't blame him because after all, this was all my fault.

He called me into the kitchen and I waited a couple of minutes, just to make it look like I wasn't listening in on the conversation. I took a couple of minutes to settle myself down and shake out all of the adrenaline I had stored up in my body. I even grabbed a towel to wipe all of the sweat from my face. I took a couple of deep breaths and slowly walked into the kitchen. I had my hands in my pocket, with my fingers crossed, just to keep up with the moment.

I walked into the kitchen, sat down on a chair, and asked him what the news was. He came right out and said, "The decision was a unanimous no". My heart sank down to my stomach and I started to feel sick. I even uncrossed my fingers because at that point, what was the use, since the final decision was a no. I didn't even know what to say, I mean, what could I even say because I was hoping this was going to be a decision in my favor. As it turned out, I was now all out of options and I had no idea what to do next.

Over the next several days, my dad went out and decided to look into other types of alternative schools. In essence schools that were designed for those who had run out of options and hit rock bottom. But after a few days of searching and speaking to some school administrators, he got some information about a continuation school.

After finally getting some positive details, he was now ready to get a plan in motion. One evening after he got home from work, he called a family meeting in the living room. I tried to keep my hopes up and for the positive, but with all of the negative results, it was hard to keep the momentum up. He explained to us that while talking to one of the administrators, he had been steered in the direction of another type of school, one which would accept any type of student. It was called a *continuation school.*

I thought to myself, “A continuation school” “What in the heck is that and where is it located?”. I knew I needed to get into a school and hoped that this would finally work itself out.

A continuation school was for students, who had various kinds of difficulties, meaning a place for those who had run out of options and nowhere else to go! I couldn’t believe it but I was now officially labeled as "one of those kids" and I never, in my wildest dreams, ever thought I was going to be classified as a troubled teenager. It was sad to say, but it was my last hope and the only choice I had left. I could only blame myself for the way this had all turned out.

With my final decision now in front of me, I was starting to get my motivation back. I was starting to feel the excitement and anticipation of getting my life back on track! This was it. I had been given my last chance and I was going to take the bull by the horns and run with it!

I told my parents; I was ready to get it done and I would do what I needed to do to move on. One of the good sides of the continuation school was they do not follow a regular semester schedule and it was a self-study type of program where students could work at their own pace.

Now I finally had a plan! I was ready and he was going to take me up to the school the next day to get registered. I was excited and ready to get the ball rolling! I got up from the couch and went into my room. I sat down at the desk to think for a couple of minutes. I needed to get my head wrapped round this because tomorrow was going to be a very busy day. I was finally back to a routine and ready to get my life back on track. All I could think of was I was going to be a high school student once again!

The next morning, I got up really early as I was excited and pumped for the day. I was dressed and ready to go, waiting in the living room for my parents as they were getting themselves ready for the day.

My new school was called Gilbert East and didn't know what to expect. I kept an eye on the drive, paying attention to where we were going so I would know how to get there. When we pulled up, I noticed the school was tucked in a corner right behind a Target store.

The only way you would notice the school was if you had seen it as you were passing by on the freeway and looked behind Target. I mean it was literally behind a shopping center! It was quiet on campus, and I didn't see anyone walking around. We walked towards the office and sat down on the chairs, waiting for our turn to talk to the principal.

After a few minutes, he came out and introduced himself to us and asked my dad a couple of questions. They were basic ones about what had happened, how everything went with Arizona and what I expected from Gilbert East. The conversation went on for a couple of minutes as we both explained our story to him and how I was sitting here in his office wanting to get my life back on track. He said he liked what he was hearing, especially when I was willing to repeat all the time I had lost and get my work done in a prompt fashion.

We talked for a little bit longer and I could tell he was on board with me getting back on track. Just as we were wrapping up our conversation, he looked at me and my dad and stated he was on board and officially granted me permission to enroll into his school. I could hardly contain my excitement because I was like, finally! It was finally time for me to get back into school! I then proceeded to ask him how the classes went and what to expect.

This was a self-study and self-paced environment; each student was to do their own work and would be graded individually as they went along with each class, meaning you would not sit in the same class and study the same material as everyone else was doing. No one studied the same work or followed the same guidelines and deadlines. It was designed that way so you could graduate quicker and get out of the work force. I again told him I was super excited and ready to start as soon as possible, even today if I could!

But that was not possible. I was required to get my previous school transcripts and immunization records. He then gave me some paperwork to fill out and bring back when I started my first day of class. We got up and thanked him and headed back to the car. I was feeling a sense of accomplishment because of all the time that had passed. Now I felt like I was not going to be wasting my time anymore. I was ready to put all of my energy in the right direction.

I immediately sat down at the table and completed the paperwork. At one point it felt like I was back in grade school getting ready for the first day of class. This was the same kind of feeling all over again. But this time around I was a teenager and much older, older in a sense of age, but as far as doing stupid things, that was a whole different topic. The feeling of excitement was now starting to kick in…

The day had finally arrived! No more sitting around and waiting for something to happen, I was getting back to school with my goal set on graduating from high school. I could really make this happen!

I now had some direction back and was gaining momentum. My compass was pointing back to the North once again after sailing south for such a long period of time. Especially after eight months of wandering aimlessly with no direction. I look back today and see how much time had flown by, wasted time, and what that can do to your mind set. It really messes with you psychologically. You sit every day and wonder if life will ever get better. You wonder and think to yourself, is this it? Is this where I am headed? Am I at the last the last stop? It really does a lot to you mentally, but all you can do is keep pushing through all of the negativity others are putting on you and more importantly, all of the negativity you put on yourself. You start to think internally, "How could I have been so stupid? How could I have done so many idiotic and dangerous things?

Eight months had given me a lot to think about and now I was prepared to move forward and chalk everything up as a learning experience. A learning experience I was never going to forget. I was super excited that I was going back to school Monday morning!

While thinking about what I was expecting of school, the one difference which was always popping up in my head was that in a continuation school, graduation had no formal ceremony like all of the normal high schools had. When you finished at Gilbert East, the principal gave you a quick handshake, handed you your diploma, and sent you on your way. No cap and gown, no celebratory walk which gave you a sense of accomplishment, none of it. You were a graduating class one of one! All you got was a slap on ass while you were on your way out the door so they can move on to the next troubled student.

I wanted to end the path of self-destruction by keeping myself focused. My head was constantly spinning with all the craziness and anticipation of what was going to happen next. I was excited and cautious all at the same time, but overall life was looking like it was on the up and up.

As we were leaving the house, my dad looked at me and asked if I was ready for this. I told him yes and I could not be more ready! We pulled up to the school, and he dropped me off. He let me know that he would be back in a few hours to pick me up. I walked through the main doors and headed inside. I had never seen anything like this before! It was almost like the whole place was in solitary confinement.

I proceeded to check in and was shown to my first class which was biology. I went up to the teacher and he explained how his classroom was organized. You worked at your own pace to get your studies done but if he felt that you were moving too slowly and not learning the material, he would stop you from where you were and send you off into another subject until you completed that one. Once you did, you were allowed to come back to his class and pick up where you left off. After a few minutes of his quick lecture, I grabbed his textbook, found an empty seat, and started to read the material.

When you heard the buzzer go off, you would move on to the next class and do the same thing, As I got up and walked into the next room, I was looking at all the other kids who were also here, but you could not tell any of them were dealing with similar issues. The only ones you could tell and were obvious were the females about eight months pregnant or had just delivered their baby!

I sat down in the next class and the buzzer went off again, so I grabbed the next book and did the same routine, read until you heard the next bell, and then move on to the next subject for the next class. Time flew by again until the last class of the day was over and I was ready to leave. I grabbed my backpack, headed out the door, and saw my dad was waiting for me in the car. I jumped in and we headed back home.

He asked me about my day, and I told him it was going to work out perfectly because of the self-paced classes and I would be done a lot quicker than normal. I then asked him how the next day was going to go with getting a ride because I needed to plan ahead. He didn't say anything until we got back home and headed inside.

As soon as I walked in, my parents presented me with a mountain bike for school so I wouldn't have to worry about getting rides all of the time. They also said it was an early present for my eighteenth birthday, which was in a few days.

I was now able to get back and forth to school without having him drop me off and picking me up every day. Obviously, there was no way I would get my driver's license anytime soon, unless I did it all on my own. Until then, there was no way I was driving a car.

I had a good feeling riding up to school because the air felt good and I was getting some nice exercise. I knew I had to keep myself motivated each day because I wanted to graduate and get on with life. Overall, it wasn't too hard to keep up the motivation, just do what you need to do and move on to the next.

The constant motivation was awesome, I felt like nothing was going to stop me from graduating this time around. I was really determined and for the first time in a long time I was excited about learning. Nothing was going to stand in my way, except for the fact I was my own worst enemy. I had always sabotaged myself one way or another for taking a short cut. If someone was going to stop me, it was going to be me and only me. I had always hindered my growth because of doing stupid things.

Life always was about my needing to feel some new type of excitement. But now that I was back on track, there was no way I was going to fall back into bad habits. There was no way I was going to let a need for excitement derail my success, or so I thought…

My eighteenth birthday was drawing closer, and I was going to become a legal adult soon. I was going to be given more latitude at school when it came to attending class, meaning I would soon find out some new rules.

It felt like it was just another day because my birthday was on a school day. I did get the happy birthday good times from my friends and family which was cool but since I was in continuation school, it was different. I wasn't too upset because, after all, I had put myself in this position to begin with and now had to deal with the consequences.

When the school got notice of me turning eighteen, the secretary called me up to the office and gave me the new updates. I did not want to go at first because I didn't want the attention for my birthday. I just wanted to get my classes done. But I went up to the office and she told me happy birthday, along with giving me the new rules. But there was one change in particular I wished she had never told me.

Being that I was an adult, I was now allowed to check myself out of school anytime I wanted to without needing a reason for it. Instantly the words "Aw Crap" came to mind! I knew myself that if I was given an inch, I would take a mile. I was going to push it because I wanted to see how much I could get away with and not get myself into too much trouble.

I just stood still for a couple of seconds and gave the secretary a deer in the headlights look because I wasn't sure I had heard her right. I asked her to repeat what she just said just to make sure.

I can call myself out of class at any time? She explained that as an adult, if you had something going on in the morning like work, medical appointment, or anything along those lines, all you had to do was call in the morning and you would be excused from class with no questions asked. Even if something had come up during the day it was still ok to call out.

It had to be a joke, right? She said those were the rules here and I was now able to use them. I looked back at her with a small cocky smile and said thanks for the information, but I did not see myself using it because I wanted to get through class and graduate. She replied and said that it was no problem but wanted to give me the information about it anyway.

I thanked her and proceeded back to class, and I started to think to myself how cool it would be to call myself out but at the same time I tried to shake it off because I knew myself and I knew I would take every advantage of that privilege.

I really wanted nothing to do with it and I wanted to put it out of my mind as quickly as I possibly could.

Stay the course I kept telling myself. *Stay on the course and get this done so you can graduate and move on with life. Keep the motivation going and keep looking ahead. Do not let your addiction get the best of you as it has so many times before.*

All I could do at this point was to stay focused for as long as I possibly could.

Chapter Nineteen

Before I knew it was Nineteen Ninety Three, and I was close to completing my junior year. School was moving along smoothly, until one day when I was getting ready for school, I grabbed my bike and hopped on. Something was a bit off, and when I looked down, I saw that my front the tire was flat. This was bad news- I had no way of getting to school.

I looked around inside the garage to see if there was a tire repair kit or something I could use to patch up the tire. I couldn't find anything I needed to fix the flat. But then an answer popped inside my head. *I could call myself out!* But I told myself that I would only do it just this one time.

So, I made the call, letting the school know I had a flat tire and within a few seconds, I was excused for the day. Right then and there I knew I was going to start down a path I didn't want to go down. Today was going to be my first official excuse to check out and this was only going to lead to more trouble. I stood still for a moment just thinking.

Did I just call myself out of class for the day? It does work! This was awesome! After all, it was only for one day and I was going to get back to class tomorrow anyway. *Just for today and today only. I won't do it again, right?*

Since Jason was at school and everyone else was gone, I had the house all to myself and time to play around. I laid down and was out in a couple of minutes. I slept for about two hours and when I got up, I went into the kitchen to make myself something to eat. I needed to get the tire fixed and was thinking of ways I can get it sealed up.

But what really consumed my thinking was this idea of checking out of class whenever I wanted. *This was going to become a problem.*

I looked around the garage but couldn't find anything to fix my tire and I finally gave up. After a while, I went back out to the garage and took the tire off to see how big the hole was. It was not very big and I had an idea that might work. I had seen a thumb tack lying around on a table. I put the thumb tack in the hole, pumped air in the tube and waited to see if it was going to stay.

Surprisingly, the tube actually stayed inflated! I carefully put the tube back into the tire and put the tire back onto the bike. After riding around for a few minutes and jumping off some curbs, my tire was still full of air. I gloated for a couple of seconds and laughed because I had plugged up a tube on my bike with a thumb tack.

Shortly afterwards I put my bike in the garage and went back inside to see what else I could do. After all I took the day off and wanted to get a couple of things done before I went back to class tomorrow. I did some laundry and cleaned up my room but mostly I just hung out for the day until everyone else got back home and I acted like nothing happened and it was just another day at school.

Before I went to bed and crashed out, I was still thinking about how easy it was to check myself out of school. I tried to put it out of my mind; I needed to stay on course and keep myself on track.

I went out to the garage to see if the thumb tack would still hold up, and, sure enough, my tire was still inflated. I jumped on and headed out to school. I jumped up and down curbs still testing to see if it would hold up and it sure was. I arrived at school and walked in expecting someone to say something to me about missing class yesterday. Not a word was said. Immediately, I put the callout idea to rest. I was looking ahead once again and getting back on track.

I felt more accomplished because of how many classes I had completed. It was around March when I walked into class and was called into the principal's office. I knew I was not in trouble because for once, I was staying out of trouble.

When I walked into the office, I sat down and the principal congratulated me on all the hard work and studying I had been doing. I had officially completed my junior year of high school and was now a senior! I could finally see the light at the end of the tunnel! I should be graduating in no time if I kept up the current pace!

I quickly headed back to class so I could get back to work. I left school and headed back home to tell my parents I just completed my junior year and was now officially a senior.

Jason's graduation was only a couple of months away. Our dad had a brief conversation while we were all hanging out in the living room and had finally put him on notice. He told Jason that once he graduated high school, his options were to get a job or go to school. Or if neither of those options had worked, our dad was going to be kicking him out of the house! I also needed to hear all of this because if this was my brothers alternative once he graduated, I could tell that this was going to be my fate as well.

I could tell Jason thought Dad was playing around, but the look on our dad's face was very serious. This was something I needed to keep in the back of my mind since I was also close to graduating.

Summer was quickly approaching along with my brother's graduation. My dad was giving Jason his constant reminder that the clock was ticking, and he had better be doing something before he graduated. But Jason's plan was the same as it had always been- play baseball and not worry about tomorrow.

Every weekend my dad warned Jason that he better have a future plan. Same result every week; he was looking for fun. Our dad suggested repeatedly that he should join the Navy because it would give him some much-needed structure, but Jason still wanted nothing to do with it. He didn't want to put any type of effort into the military. He still just wanted a simple life. He had to be pushed to get something done like filling out a job application. Now with just thirty days away.

I was actually getting nervous for Jason because our dad wasn't playing around, and I could see he was on the brink of his boiling point! This had actually worked out well for me because I was in the shadows and keeping a low profile. For once, my brother was the focus of attention. I told him I would not be surprised if he gave him the boot once he graduated.

I went to school the next day and asked around to see if there were any jobs available for the summer since I had a few months off and didn't want to be at the house. It was crazy timing because one of the teachers informed me of a work program Gilbert East offered to senior students.

He pulled me aside and explained many of the businesses in the area were looking for students to work over the summer and they would pay them minimum wage with the possibility of raises.

This was perfect! I was going to be getting my first job ever! He then gave me some paperwork to fill out and I needed to bring it back to school as soon as possible before the start date. I did not have to do an interview because they were looking for students recommended by the teachers, which made the process a lot easier. I would be applying for a job at a race car track. This was going to work out perfectly!

I grabbed my bike and flew back home so I could tell my parents I was getting a job for the summer. I rushed inside the house, sat down in the kitchen, and filled out the paperwork. I tore through the pages and filled out everything as fast as I could. I had adrenaline pumping throughout my body because this was going to be my first job ever!

I made sure the application was filled out correctly. I left the house feeling good and headed off to school. When I arrived and put my bike in the rack, I found the teacher and gave him the paperwork.

He took it and said I should be getting a call shortly from the manager of the track. I thanked him and headed off to class. The day flew by and I headed home. When I got back my mom asked me how the position looked, and I told her I was waiting to hear from the boss. She was hoping for the best.

After several days of waiting, I finally got the call from the manager. We had a quick phone interview, and I was asked some basic questions. This was going to be a full-time position over the summer. He also let me know if I wanted to stay on for a longer period of time, he had the authority to extend employment beyond the summer.

I told him everything sounded good and I asked when he needed me to start. He said once school was out, I had the position locked in and he congratulated me. I hung up the phone and I let my mom know I got the position and was going to start once school was out. She was excited because I was completing high school and now had my first full time job! I was excited about the direction my life was taking! Not having any need for an adrenaline rush or the impulse to do something stupid was a fantastic feeling!

My life was getting more interesting because I was actually doing well and currently staying out of trouble.

My brother, on the other hand, was the one going to be graduating and time had finally caught up to him. He had to become a part of the working class and be a part of society. One who pays into the tax system and works a nine to five job for the next thirty years until he retires at age sixty-five and heads off into his golden years, with social security, and then dies.

Graduation was upon him but alas, he had no clue what he was going to do with his life. It was no shocker to anyone that he had not come to any decision.

He had his graduation ceremony over the weekend which included the walk, diploma, and the tossing of the cap in the air and everything else that went along with a high school graduation. He even got a congratulation bag from the family which had some good stuff in it; he got a watch, lots of cash and some other stuff I can't remember. He also got the graduation party from our parents, the whole works.

At that moment, I wondered if I was going to get something like he got for my graduation? I mean I was in a high school, after all, but not a typical high school. I knew I was not going to be having all of the graduation fluff because of where I was going.

Mine was going to be a plain and simple a handshake, swift kick on the bum, diploma in my hand, and straight out the door! Right through the turn style so I can take a number and pass right on by into the working world.

Jason had it all for his graduation; all I could do was sit back and watch. I knew it was never going to be me and had accepted the fact I was never going to be one of those who would have a high school graduation. All because of wanting to push my boundaries for a quick adrenaline rush.

As quickly as the celebration had started, it had come to a screeching halt. That's when my dad changed the clear skies filled with rainbows and roses, to one with dark clouds and a chance of a hurricane. Everyone was having a good time when he turned and told my brother he had until Monday to make a final decision.

All Jason did was smile and nod his head. He was so wrapped up in his graduation he didn't even listen to a word Dad was saying! All Jason cared about at that point in time was that he graduated and high school was well behind him.

My dad said his piece and let Jason enjoy his time with the graduation festivities for the time being. Jason then called a couple of his friends and they all went out for the night to celebrate. I went to hang out in my room for the night as everything was winding down. Jason had the entire weekend to get something together, but he just kept on having a good time celebrating.

But Monday quickly arrived! It was going to be the day of reckoning.

Dad came into our room and woke Jason up nice and early. He stood over Jason while he was lying in bed and looked him straight in the eyes and asked him what he was going to do. Jason said he didn’t know, so my dad made him get up out of bed, get changed and go out to the living room.

I could see in his face that he had no clue what was going to happen next. He took his time getting changed and tried to milk every second he could by going as slow as possible before he headed to the living room. I sat quietly in bed not saying a word because I didn’t want to make anything worse.

I had all kinds of scenarios swirling through my head as I could see the exact same thing happening to me once I graduated high school. I didn’t want to be stuck like he was with no sense of direction so I needed to get myself a gameplan together and make something happen.

When Jason went into the living room, he sat down on the couch and dad asked him again what he was going to be doing with his life. My brother replied with the same words - he didn’t know what he was going to do. This was it; this was what everything had come down to!

After a short conversation, our dad looked at him straight in the eyes once again and told him to pack his bags because he was kicking him out! It was as if all of the air had been sucked out of the house in that one brief moment. I was trying to process what I had just heard because my head was spinning in circles! Did he really just kick him out of the house, I thought?

Jason didn't process what our dad had just said and thought it was a joke so he looked back at him and said "*right, watch how fast I go*". Our mom, who was sitting right next to him and had a look of seriousness on her face. She had a good poker face because you could never really tell what she was thinking or going to say. Which made it even worse in this situation because you couldn't tell what she was going to say to Jason.

When she finally did say something, she also looked Jason straight in the eye and said the same thing as time was up and had to move on because he could not make up his mind on what he was going to be doing in life.

Damn! I could not believe both of them actually did it! They were serious about all of this! I instantly sprang out of bed and went out to the hallway, just so I could listen more closely to the conversation. I wanted to get every detail and make sure I knew what was being said.

Jason sat there quietly and motionless as all he could do was stare back at them in disbelief. He had the look of a deer in headlights on his face as he was trying to process what had just been said. Our parents had just dropped a bomb on him and he was totally shocked. After all they did give him plenty of time to decide so this was not a sudden notice.

Our dad stood over him and told him once again he needed to get his bags and get out. He had given him all that time in the world and he didn't take anything seriously. So, they figured this was the best way to get him motivated and they meant business.

I could see my brother get up from the couch and once he did, I quickly ran back into the bedroom and jumped back into bed. I didn't want him to know I had heard the entire conversation. Jason came back into our room and stood in the middle of the bedroom shaking. I couldn't tell if he was pissed, nervous or anxious. Or maybe a bit of all three! So, he packed up a small bag, called James and headed over to his house.

Not much was said as he walked out the door. They all looked at each other as if it were a wild west showdown! Who was going to blink first and say something as he walked out the door!

The tension was getting crazy because no one knew really what to say because this was all happening so fast. In the end, they all just made eye contact and said nothing as Jason walked out the door. I really thought this was going to turn into a screaming and shouting match but it ended up being a quite situation as Jason walked out. I guess they all wanted this to be done with and move on with life.

After all was said and done, I sat for a moment thinking, I was now going to be in the same boat as he was when I graduate and I needed to prepare myself for what was going to happen to me in the near future. The difference was I was way ready to move on with life and get out of the house! More and more the idea of joining the Navy played over and over in my head.

My dad had mentioned it to my brother on several occasions as he said, "If nothing else, the Navy can be the start of getting your life in order". After all, our dad served in the Navy for four years, so he should know what he was talking about.

Could I see myself going into the armed forces? At this point, I was willing to put the idea on the table and give it a serious thought.

Once Jsaon walked out of the house, my dad closed the door and said, "Jason was not allowed to step one foot in the house". I guess it was because they were making a point. It felt kind of funny at first because I was at the house by myself! I always wanted to get on with my life and be on my own, always counting down the days until I graduated. I was always looking forward to that day because of how I felt about school; I just wanted to get it done and graduate.

After my parents left, I headed out over to James's house.

I asked my brother what his game plan was going to be, and he said he had no idea, as if he didn't really care. Right after his statement he asked the both of us if we wanted to go play baseball. We both looked at Jason as if he were crazy!

James explained to him the whole reason he was staying at his house was because he got kicked out for not having a plan and now he wanted to go play baseball? We both said it was a bad idea because of how many problems it had already created. I didn't want to stick around because of how this whole situation went down in the first place.

I now had to focus on myself. Jason had made his decisions and now had to deal with them as he sees fit. I needed to get my own sense of direction as well because I didn't want to end up the same way. After all I did have something positive going for me in the way of now going to my first job! So, I walked back home thinking of how I was going to prepare myself for my first day of work at the track.

This was something I was really looking forward to as it could springboard me in the right direction.

Chapter Nineteen

I peddled as fast as I could because I wanted to get myself into a good mindset before I arrived. Since it was going to be my first day, I didn't want anything messing it up.

When I checked in, I was directed to go to the back room and ask for Jackson. I went up to him and he introduced himself and immediately asked if I was ready to get started since I was recommended from Gilbert East. Excitedly, I replied yes, and he handed me some basic paperwork. Once it was all completed, I went right to work. I was told to look for a guy named Daniel, who was to be my supervisor.

I went out to the track and saw a tallish guy with a crazy looking mullet standing by himself. I told him I was the new employee, Eric, and I would be working with him. He then proceeded to show me around the place and explained what some of my duties would entail, like starting up the cars in the morning, along with other basic responsibilities. I knew this job was going to be a lot of work and a lot of fun all at the same time.

At the end of the day, I was dirty, smelled like a mule, and was totally exhausted, but also feeling a sense of accomplishment! It felt good to have my first job.

When I got back home my mom asked me how the day went and I told her it was great and was going to be a lot of fun working there for the summer. It was the same routine on my second day, and I was also introduced to another supervisor named Donald. He was quite young and was working two jobs at the same time to support his wife and young son. He married young and decided to finish his senior year of high school while working in two places full time. When I first got to know him, he was very reserved and only spoke when he needed something done.

He was not much for small talk and really focused on his work. Jackson informed me that Donald was another supervisor when he was not around. If anything were to happen, I had to report to him directly.

I checked in with Donald and introduced myself to him. He then sent me over to Daniel so we could get to work. Occasionally the two of them would butt heads because of the supervisor title. Daniel only wanted to report to Jackson and found it difficult to report to Donald. It was also hard for me sometimes too because Daniel was my supervisor and when Daniel told me to do something, Donald stepped in and gave me something different to do. This always pissed Daniel off.

I just went along with the flow and did what I was told; sometimes I had to split myself in half because of the different directions I was given. However, it was ok with me because overall I had good supervisors and if the job was getting done, that's all anyone was concerned about.

We had a great bunch of guys and I couldn't ask for anything better for my first job! It was so much fun. At the end of every shift, we were allowed to race around the track in order to attract other customers who were coming off the streets and buying tickets.

Every day when we got off work, we would do some driving and race some of the other customers. At the same time, we were building repeat business because we would talk to the costumers and invite them back as often as possible to race against us. In essence, not only were we working on the track but we were also in sales because of all the new customers we were attracting. It was working out great and this went on for weeks.

I learned a lot from Daniel and Donald. Their personalities and leadership skills differed from each other but their combined skills on the management side of the business seemed successful.

On a rare occasion we had some days with absolutely nothing to do because we didn't have many customers. It was during these times I needed to get some type of rush because I was bored and wanted to keep the excitement of the new job going.

One particular day, a couple of customers came inside to ride around the track. They raced each other around several times and wanted to keep going. Just when I figured everything was going great, ideas started spinning inside my head. As soon as the riders said they were finished and needed to go and buy more tickets, my mind instantly formulated a plan on how I could get paid something extra on the side and collect my regular paycheck.

When a customer bought their book of tickets to ride, it cost them about twenty dollars for their time, with each one lasting about three to five minutes depending on how many people were on the track. Once they handed me the tickets, I would take the tickets and put them in an open metal box that was sitting on the side of the track.

At the end of the day, we would take out the tickets from the box and toss them away in a big dumpster. Just when I was putting the tickets inside the metal box, I had a crazy thought-*does anyone really count the tickets as they were put inside the box throughout the day?* Who keeps track of all that? That's when I scouted out the entire process, from putting the tickets inside the box, watching how they were monitored, and at the end of the day how they were disposed of.

I learned how the entire process worked for disposing of the tickets and I was ready to implement *my plan*. As a test run, I tried it out on a couple of regular customers who were frequently at the track. When they bought their tickets and started their race, I would take one of their tickets and put it inside the box while I would take another ticket and put it inside my pocket.

When I accumulated 10 tickets, I asked the regulars if they wanted to "buy" some at a discount. I could sell them tickets at half price. Instantly their eyes would light up with just the thought of getting the tickets for ten dollars! I told them they didn't even have to get out of the cars once they were finished.

The regulars were totally in, so I pulled out the tickets from my pocket and sold them back for the "discounted price." It was a win, win for the both of us because they got discounted tickets, and I got paid some extra cash on the side. They continued to go around the track several times and as they were finishing up, I told them to ask me for the tickets every time they came down to the track.

They loved the idea.

I had figured out a way I could get some extra cash! It was full proof! I also knew if I were to get caught by anyone, I would be fired right on the spot. But the key was not to be greedy and to know who I was selling my tickets to. Throughout the day many more riders were coming onto the track, and I started to feel out the riders to whom I could sell tickets and the ones I needed to walk away from.

By the end of my shift, I had built my list of people who I knew I could sell tickets to and create a cash making machine! I also created a new form of excitement, which actually meant a lot more to me then the money did.

I was cleaning up with how much money I was making from the extra tickets. I was getting my regular paycheck and, on the side, collecting cash from selling the extra tickets. Every sale was a potential to be fired, which made me want to push my plan even further!

Some of the employees at the track were wondering why I was talking to so many of the customers. So, I started to screen out the other employees as to whom I could also trust to cut in on the action. There was one employee who needed some help because he was in a bind and picking up as many shifts as he could. I told him I had a way that could help him out with some extra cash.

As the customers were coming off the track and about to ride, I showed him how I was making money with the tickets and how well it was going. More specifically, I spelled out the keys to not getting popped-*don't get too greedy, keep it simple when you select your customers, constantly look around to see if anyone was listening to your conversation, and don't keep too many tickets in your possession*. I told him if he followed those rules, he wouldn't get caught.

He then started to get into the game but for whatever reason, this guy would not listen to what I told him.

He started off small but after a few days of getting to know how the system worked, he saw the cash coming in fast and started to get greedy with the tickets. He was stashing more and more tickets each day in his pockets, I told him to only keep a few tickets at a time in case something happened and he got caught.

Well, after ignoring my every warning, trouble finally caught up to him.

When I was coming in for a later shift, he was getting off and called me over. He said he wanted to show me something and when he opened up his backpack, he had a stack of tickets piled up inside it! I mean like hundreds of tickets! I looked at him as if he was crazy and told him straight out, "You have way too many tickets in your possession and you're playing a dangerous game."

Even with the amount of risk I was always willing to take, I knew he was on the verge of getting caught. He didn't care because as long as he was making money, that was all that mattered to him.

I told him to be careful with those tickets because if he gets caught with them, he'd be fired right on the spot, but more importantly, he'd be screwing up my entire system!

This guy really didn't seem to care and went on about business as usual. After seeing his backpack, I started to carry less of the tickets on me just in case something happened with this guy.

Well, it finally happened that the ticket trail caught up to him. Within a few days of him being on the job, he got caught trying to sell one of the customers some of the tickets, someone had seen him reaching inside his backpack and taking out some tickets. When one of the supervisors told him to open his backpack up so they could look inside, they saw the stacks of tickets and fired him right on the spot!

After he was fired the consequences rained on every employee at the track. Supervisors were now monitoring all the tickets being put inside the metal box and collected them at the end of every shift. All of the extra cash I was making was now officially over because one person decided to get too greedy and had taken down the system I created! I was a bit pissed at first because the extra cash I made on the side was gone, but I still held on to my job.

He did not take anyone else down when he got caught, and he left quietly. I learned from the start to never take any tickets home with me and never start my shift with any in my possession just in case I was called out and searched.

Nothing ever serious came down on me and I put the whole ordeal behind me as quickly as it started. My money making system had been officially shut down. Once management cleaned up the tickets mess, we all went back to work like business as usual.

It was only a matter of time before summer ended and I was back in school. I had a lot of fun working at the track and was wondering if they were going to keep me on after the summer was over. Since the season was going to be changing soon, I was not sure how many employees they were going to keep on.

All I could do from that point was take it day by day.

I just had to deal with what was in front of me and not dwell on it.

Chapter Twenty

My brother, Jason, finally had to decide what he was going to do going forward. He was just about out of money and was running out of options. He had finally had the realization that life as moving forward and decided he was going to enlist in the Navy. With that being said, our dad allowed him to come back to the house as long as he was studying for the Armed Services Vocational Aptitude Battery test.

Jason explained that he was ready but the only thing holding him back was he had no idea where to find a recruiting station. I don't know if he used it as a ploy for buying more time, but our dad was having nothing to do with any of it! There was no way he was going to let him just sit around and use it as an excuse.

Dad was moving like lightning, calling around and getting numbers to every recruiter's office. It was almost comical – he was so obsessed with getting Jason to go straight into the military, no ifs, ands, or buts. Jason's time had run out.

After making a couple of calls, he found a recruitment office that was close by. It was time for Jason to get ready to go, and Dad was waiting by the door. I loved every minute of it. The attention was off me (again) and right back on to him! But it was only a matter of time for me once I graduated high school; I would be in the same position as my brother, which was fine with me. I always liked my independence and wanted to be on my own once I graduated. I didn't need to be pushed out.

I called James to let him know that when Jason got back to the house, he was basically hauled off to the Navy recruitment office and he looked like he had just been arrested. Jason was finally getting his life together, and this was the best thing that could have happened to him.

After a few hours of waiting, they received the information regarding what he was going to be doing. I was curious as to what kind of job he qualified for and when he would be heading out to basic training. When they returned, questions were burning through my mind and just as I was about to ask, my dad announced that Jason did not get in!

Wait a minute, how did he not make it in? Well, Jason didn't score high enough on the ASVB test and he really needed to study. He had to wait a month to take the test again. Jason could stay at the house if he were willing to study for the test and try again to get a passing score.

All Jason had to do was to study for the ASVB and get the highest score possible for his new job. It had worked out perfectly for him and it also worked out on my side too because as long as he as studying and I was in school plus working, everything would continue to stay quiet, and all would be all right with the world.

Chapter Twenty-One

After an early shift, I called James to see what he was doing. He told me that a friend of his was having a birthday party and there were going to be drinks there as well. I let him know I could not be out too late since the track was having a professional race and sponsors would be covering the event.

In the back of my mind, I was thinking this was probably a bad idea and may extend into a longer night than expected. But, on the other hand, I couldn't pass up the opportunity of drinking. I started off with a couple of drinks and introduced myself to everyone. I reiterated that I had a long day ahead of me tomorrow and needed to keep in control for the night.

After about an hour of eating and drinking, I was feeling good, but I knew with my addictive personality, it was looking less and less likely that I would be leaving anytime soon.

Our friend, who drove us up to the party had hit his limit with drinking, but of course, it didn't stop me from continuing. I was having drink after drink and then saw the hard alcohol. My heart was pumping and the next thing I knew I was grabbing a bottle of Southern Comfort and taking one shot after another. It's been many years ago when this happened, and I can still taste that stuff!

Instantly, all the shots hit me like a ton of bricks, and in a matter of minutes I was wobbling all over the place. I was slurring my speech and when I started to talk, I could not even get my words out. I had hit the point of no return and didn't even know where I was.

I continued drinking everything that was poured in my cup, but it was coming out the sides of my mouth and dribbling down my chin. I looked over at James and we both started to laugh because I could barely stand up. I told James I was not feeling well. I was losing my balance and couldn't even sit down straight without falling over. That's when I blacked out and I have no recollection of what happened after I sat down.

Once this happened, the night was officially called. They took me by the shoulders and got me into the car, putting me in the back seat. I don't remember much of what happened from that point on.

After pulling up in front of my house, I got out of the car and took a couple of steps before I fell over. My motor skills were not functioning, and I literally just fell down as I was walking to the front door. I was able to get my hands in my pocket to get my keys out and open the front door open. I felt like I had to throw up and was in the bathroom for what felt like a couple of hours.

Once I felt a bit better, I hopped up, headed straight to the bedroom, and tore my clothes off so I could jump right into bed. I crashed right away and knew it was going to be extremely hard for me to get up in the morning, but I had to do whatever it took to get myself out of bed and up for work.

Luckily, I had set my alarm for the right time and set a backup time just in case I couldn't get up for the first one. Within a couple of hours, my first alarm went off and sounded really loud but I was so out of it I slept straight through it. I was snoring very loudly, apparently because of the dehydration and it drowned out the sound of the alarm.

Once the second alarm went off, I had to get myself out of bed because if I didn't, there would be no way I was going to get to work on time, or for that matter get to work at all. I started to slap myself around to wake up and my head started to thump as if someone was beating on it like a drum. I had a major hangover. I couldn't even swallow my own saliva because I was so dry.

I looked myself over and saw some bruises. I had no idea how I got them and I didn't have time to figure it out because the clock was ticking. I had to come up with a reason for being late for work- my bike! *It had a flat tire and there was no way I could fix it.* I had to get a new tube because the whole was too big to fix.

After about eight rings someone answered. Luckily it was Donald, and I was jumping for joy because Donald was a lot easier to talk to then Jackson. I gathered myself together and with all the energy I could muster, I started to tell him that as I was riding to work my tire had blown out and I had to get a new one. I also told him I was working as fast as I could to get it repaired and once I did, I was on my way straight up to the track.

Don said it was ok but I needed to get up to the track as fast as possible. I told him I would be out the door shortly and would be heading up as quickly as I could. I hung up the phone and bought myself a little bit more time. I headed straight for the shower, got dressed and headed out the door.

I saw my dad sitting on the couch and was not sure what to say, so I hurried past him and said I was running a little bit behind. He gave me a smirk but didn't say a word. I didn't know if it was a good or a bad thing, but it didn't matter to me at that point because all I was concerned about was getting straight to work.

Still reeling from my hangover, I was peddling so fast I didn't even think about the headache. After about a twenty-minute bike ride I finally made it to work.

With all the commotion going on, I couldn't put my bike inside the garage like I normally did or lock it up outside the gate because I didn't want anyone to see me coming in, especially Jackson.

I found Donald, and checked in. I tried to talk to him as little as possible because I knew I was reeking of alcohol and did not want anyone to know the reason I was late was because of a hangover. So, I stayed as quiet as possible and kept as much distance from all the supervisors as I could. I jumped right out on the track to monitor the races. I kept it cool as if nothing had ever happened and I was there for the beginning race.

Wow! I actually did it! I knew it was going to be a long day from this point on as my body was hurting and my head was still pounding, but the most important part was I made it into work and did my job.

I went along with what everyone else was doing for the races without getting close to anyone. Everything was going well until about an hour from the last race. The place was packed with people, cars were spinning around on the track, and everyone was having a great time. I looked around to make sure everything was under control and when I looked out to see how my bike was doing, I noticed that a small mini truck had pulled up next to my bike. It took only a split second when two guys jumped out of the truck and tossed my bike in the back. It happened so fast that by the time I saw them putting my bike in the back of the truck, it was too late. I yelled out, "Stop, they're stealing my bike!"

Daniel heard me and scrambled to his car, jumped in, and took off after them like a bat out of hell. I couldn't get a description of the truck because of how fast everything had happened. From this point on all I could do was hope and wait until Daniel got back.

Jackson came over to see what was going on and I explained to him that two guys had just taken off with my bike. He asked me why I parked outside the gate and I had to think quickly. I couldn't tell him I came to work late because of a night of heavy drinking resulting in a hangover.

So, I concocted what I thought was a believable excuse. *I thought my bike would take up too much room inside the garage and the track would need the room for the cars and the people from the races. So, I thought it would be a good idea if I parked it outside the track.*

He apparently believed me, but told me that from now on, no matter what was going on at the track, I needed to put my bike inside the garage. We went back to business, and I waited for Daniel to come back with news of my bike. After a few minutes, Daniel returned but there was no sign of my bike. I couldn't see anything; I asked him what happened and he said he went as fast as he could but he couldn't catch up to them.

I was so pissed, mostly at myself because if I had not gotten hammered the night before, I would have parked my bike in the garage. This whole ordeal could have been prevented and I would still have my bike. Chalk this one up to doing something stupid, like so many times before. I now had no bike, hung over from a night of drinking, and now had to worry about how I was going to get back home. I also had to think about how I was going to be getting to work for the rest of the summer.

Daniel offered to drop me off when our shift was over, and I couldn't wait to leave. This entire day was karma for the stupid stuff I had previously done while working there.

As the day was ending, the racers were starting to exit the track and head home for the night. Daniel and I clocked out and I hopped into his car, and we proceeded to head back to my house. Daniel started to ask me if things were going to be ok and I had told him it was going to be cool, but I had to explain to my dad how the bike got stolen. I thanked Daniel for the ride and told him I would see him first thing in the morning.

When I finally got home, I prepared myself for what my dad was going to say and was ready for any questions he would have. When I walked through the front door, my dad was on the couch looking straight at me and right before he could say a word, I had shouted out, "My bike got stolen today."

He fired back, "How the hell did your bike get stolen when you were at work?"

I went on to explain how I woke up late and when I rushed off to work there was a big race going on and I didn't want to interfere with the race. I had locked my bike up outside the gate along a fence to make it easier for me to get to work. He looked at me and just shook his head back and forth then said, "Way to go kid."

I asked him how I was going to get to work tomorrow, so he said, "Use your mothers bike since she was taking the bus to work." It was after all just sitting in the back yard. So, for the time being, I would be taking her bike to work. I had taken myself down the drinking path too many times already and I was still only a teenager.

For the rest of the night, I told myself I would never drink like that again because I was out of control, and it had cost me my bike. It could have been a lot worse but overall, I got lucky.

I realized that drinking was not worth all of the aggravation and swore it off forever…

Chapter Twenty-Two

Daniel and I were the first ones to check in for the morning and were responsible for opening. When I pulled up, I headed straight to the garage and parked the bike as far back as I could. I even found a small tarp to put over it to hide it from everyone. I was riding a lady's bike! This would be another consequence of what had happened the night before. Little by little I was seeing the end results of my actions.

I was hoping no one would see it because these guys lived for busting each other's chops and once they knew they had something on you, it would be an all - day event. I knew I would be facing the consequences after what happened with the drinking, but at least this time, it wouldn't be anything too severe.

When I went into the office to clock in, Daniel asked me if everything had turned out okay from last night and told him I was able to get a hold of a bike for the time being. He asked if I had parked it inside the garage this time and told him it was safe and sound inside. We kept our conversation short and went right to work.

Daniel and I were out on the track taking care of business and I was constantly peeking inside the garage to see if anyone was poking around under the tarp. It was hard trying to do my job and make sure the bike would stay covered because I would be in for it the minute, they found it.

About halfway through the day, someone needed to get in the very back of the garage and get some oil for one of the cars. As they were inching their way back, they reached the tarp and decided to take it off to move it out of the way. The bike was now uncovered, and they wanted to know whose it was because there were no girls working out on the track except the ones who worked in the front office.

All I could do was keep quiet and hope no one else would say anything. Then I heard Daniel shouting, "Whose bike is this?" As soon as Daniel walked over to look, he blurted out, "The only one who had a bike back there was Eric!"

Shit! The cat was now out of the bag! He walked over to take a closer look and when he saw what color it was, he started to laugh. He called out my name and asked if it was mine. Shaking my head reluctantly I yelled back, "Yes, it's mine! Go ahead, get it out of your system."

The word was out, and Daniel was still laughing and saying, "You actually rode this up here?" When the moment presented itself to give someone a hard time, nothing was spared at anyone's expense.

For the rest of the day, I had to prepare myself for all of the bad jokes which were headed my way. Everyone was coming up to me asking the same question with smiles on their faces, but everyone knew it was all for fun, and there was no harm in what we were doing. Hell, if it were someone else, I would have done the exact same thing to them! It was no problem with getting razzed because it was all fun.

By the end of the day when I was ready to clock out, I heard it from everyone at the track. I mean Jackson even got in on the running joke too. He figured since he was the boss it was his duty to join in the fun. I was dreading going into the garage and grabbing the bike.

Standing in front of me were Daniel and a couple of the others whooping as I walked over to get the bike. They were all smiling and laughing so I just jumped on the bike, and they were all still laughing hysterically as I rode off. All I could do was laugh and waive as I peddled off from the track. I headed back home laughing because everyone had a good laugh at my expense; it was all fun and overall, a fun day. I hoped that everyone had gotten it out of their system.

On my next day at work, nothing more was said about the bike situation, and everyone turned their attention to their duties. Summer was drawing to a close, with only about a week left, and school was starting soon. I knew I couldn't continue working full time and wondered when I was going to be told what was going to happen with my schedule.

Jackson called me into his office. He started to explain to me I had done a great job over the summer and that he and Daniel were really satisfied with my job performance. With all that in mind, he asked me if I wanted to keep working on the weekends and the nighttime once school started,

Wow! He was willing to keep me on beyond summertime! I told him I would be glad to take on the extra shifts and would have no problem in doing so. He got up, shook my hand, and thanked me. He then said, "Get back to work and I will be calling you with your new work schedule."

I went back outside and continued as usual. I told Daniel about my meeting with Jackson, and he told me that he was happy to work with me because of all the fun we had, and when push came to shove, we always got the job done, even if it was just the two of us out on the track for the day. At the end of my shift, I saw

Jackson then filled out some new paperwork for the continued work program and then headed back home.

I went into the house and told my parents that, when the summer was over, Jackson was willing to keep me on for the weekends and weeknights. It was a small victory for me after all that's happened!

My parents were both good with the idea as long as I was back in school and completing my schoolwork. The only thing I had to worry about was getting a new bike because I was still riding my mom's bike. There was no way I was taking Mom's bike up to Gilbert East!

I reached out to a friend of mine who had a few BMX bikes sitting around and asked him if I could borrow one of them until I got a new one. I now had a bike for school and I could focus my attention back on what I needed to do.

Chapter Twenty-Three

I felt like I was making some great strides and needed to keep it going. I was finally back on track and now on solid ground starting my senior year. Before I knew it the weeks were flying by, and I was knocking out classes one by one. My list of required classes was getting shorter and shorter. Everything was going well, maybe too well, which kind of worried me…

Once I knew I was on the right path, I always found a way to sabotage myself because I always felt life was going all too well. I really wanted to push through and complete these classes even more quickly.

So, I came up with an idea and with some clever thinking, found an easy solution which would help me graduate a lot faster. Working every weekend as well as the weeknights was starting to catch up to me. As I was sitting in class one morning I was starting to crash out. I had to figure out a way where I could stay home without my parents noticing, just so I can catch up with some sleep. I quickly formulated a plan. I would get dressed and head out to the garage. I would stay there until my parents left for work. I knew how much time I would need to stay in the garage until they both were gone.

When it was all clear, I would open the door back up, put the lock back on and go back inside the house. I then called the secretary to let her know I needed to check myself out for the day because I had to go to work. My plan worked like a charm! After I called in, I got undressed and went back to bed. Jason also crashed out and didn't hear a thing.

The next day, nothing was said, of course, and it was business as usual. I was thinking to myself, if it was this easy to take a day off, I wondered how far I could push this? I didn't *want* to sabotage myself, as I always had done, but this was too easy. I would think of different ways to use the time off.

Week after week went by and Jason was now ready to retake his ASVAB test. Everyone in the house was super excited that he was finally going to retake the test and we were all hoping he would score high enough to get in.

On the day of the test, our dad drove Jason back down to the recruiter's office. When they returned home, our dad yelled out, "He passed!" He scored high enough and finally got accepted into the Navy!

I asked him when he was leaving for basic training. He said he would be leaving for San Diego within the next few weeks, and he'd be there for about three months. He had mixed emotions. He wanted to leave but at the same time he wanted to stay home and needed to get that extra push. But now that he had a date when he was going to be officially leaving, he would be out and about until his time at home was up.

Over the next couple of days, I called the school and excused myself from class. I figured since I would be the only one at home, I could have the house to myself and hang out without having to worry about anyone being here.

On one of the days, I had called out, something interesting happened. I don't know if it was sheer coincidence, but when I was at home, there was a knock at the door and for some reason I thought it might be important. I had after called myself out of class and was technically ditching for the day. I thought to myself, "Had someone from the school been sent over to my house to check on me?" I began to get really nervous and my heart started to pound inside my chest because it could have been anyone, especially someone from the school!

I quietly approached the door trying to not make a sound, landing every footstep with the least amount of pressure so as to not make any type of squeaking noise on the floor. It was as if I was trying to fly across the hallway in a single leap and keep myself afloat as I was grabbing on to the door.

When I got to the door, I kept as much distance as I could from myself and the doorway, just so the other person couldn't see my shadow on the ground, or even hear me breathing for that matter! At this point, I couldn't afford to take any chances and needed to be as invisible as possible.

I finally propped myself up and looked through the peep hole to see who it was, all the while I was holding my breath and shaking with anticipation. There standing in front of the door was a Navy uniform. I instantly let out a huge sigh of relief! I slowly calmed myself down and got my breathing back to normal. I knew he wasn't there for me and could finally relax for a moment.

"Anyone from the Navy must be looking for Jason and not me." I said to myself. I got myself back into the right state of mind and was ready to see what they wanted.

I unlocked the door and as I opened it, he looked at me and asked, "Is Jason around? There is some important paperwork for him I need for him to sign." I looked at him and asked, "Is there something specifically you needed from him, because he was out running some errands and would be back later." He then gave me some papers for Jason to fill out and said, "I need them back as soon as possible because they were very important." More importantly I asked who he was and he told me, "I am Jason's recruiter and following up on his progress." I grabbed the paperwork from him and I let him know I would hand them off once I saw him.

Just as I was about to close the door, he asked me, "Were you home from school today from being sick?" "Not particularly" I said back, more so, "I am trying to figure out some things on where I want to be once I finished High School."

After a couple minutes of talking, he asked me, "How much longer do you have left until you graduate?" I told him, "I didn't actually know because I was in continuation school and it was hard to give a specific answer." More so I told him, "There was no specific graduation date since we all worked at a different pace from each other."

I was trying to wrap the conversation up as quickly as I could because I wanted to get back inside. Just as I was about to turn around and close the door, he reached into his pocket and pulled out his business card. He asked, "Do you have any specific plans once you graduate?" I told him, "I didn't because I wanted to focus on getting my diploma first and then look at where I wanted to be headed."

I took his card, and he mentioned, "You can call me at any time if you ever have any questions about the possibility of getting ahead, or if you ever wanted an opportunity to enlist in the Navy, to see what opportunities they can give you." I took his card, put it in my pocket and thanked him for stopping by. I then closed the door and went back to bed not even thinking about our conversation, or even if there was any potential with his offer. It was something that I would seriously consider.

Jason returned shortly after, and I gave him the papers. I also told him he needed to get them back to the recruiter as soon as possible. After he looked them over, he bolted out the door with a friend and headed back to the recruiter's office.

Time was ticking by, and Jason was only a few days away from leaving for basic training. He was getting nervous and you could see all over his face that he wanted nothing to do with the Navy. He was hanging out with everyone and anyone as much as possible because he wanted to get as much packed in before he left for the next three months.

When this clock had finally run out, the special moment arrived. His recruiter stopped by early in the morning and Jason was officially off to basic training! We watched as he faded away into the morning light and after all of the excitement had calmed down, my dad looked over at me and the first thing he said was, "You're next buddy! You better start thinking about what you're going to be doing because your time is also coming."

Once Jason left for basic training, I decided I might investigate what options were available for me and I thought that I might even consider enlisting in the Navy! At that point anything was possible. I never had any problem with the idea of moving out and being on my own, but I needed to graduate high school first before I could do anything.

More and more I was thinking about what my brother's recruiter had said about giving him a call, just to see what my options were.

Over the next couple of months, I was calling myself out of school more often then I should have. I knew I was pushing my luck as something negative was bound to happen. In the beginning, I was getting excited when I called out from school as well as from hiding that fact from my family. But it had come to the point where I did not even get up to go out and do my morning school routine because I had gotten lazy. Calling myself out of school had become boring.

I figured I would sleep in and skip my whole routine, just to see how much farther I could push this. What I did not plan on though was that my dad had taken the day off as well and also decided to sleep in! By now it was too late for me to get up and get to the garage because if I opened the front door, he would have heard me, and I would have been caught.

Immediately I hit the "OH CRAP!" panic button! I had to think of a way to get outside or hide myself until my dad left the house. I did the only thing I could possibly do which was to slowly creep out of bed, grab my blanket, and hide under the bed. I knew this was going to be a long shot, but if he had come into the room and found me there, all hell would have broken loose!

I grabbed my blanket and hid under the bed. I covered myself up from head to toe and didn't make a sound. I slowed my breathing to a minimum to stay as quiet as I could. I was all nice and secure under the bed when I heard him get up and head down the hallway. For whatever reason, he passed my bedroom and decided to peek inside. It was hard to say exactly why but all I knew was I heard him standing at the doorway looking into the room.

He did notice, however, that my blanket was underneath the bed and because he saw it, he went over and turned the bedroom light on to get a better look. My heart was pounding a mile a minute! I was feeling myself sweat buckets of water because it was so hot underneath the blankets. I took short, shallow breaths and was truly surprised he couldn't hear my heart pounding through my chest, it seemed that loud.

He did a quick look over and stood there for a couple more minutes. I was thinking he was waiting for some type of movement, but I continued to stay still. I knew once I made even the slightest motion it would be game over.

Finally, when he convinced himself there was nothing under the bed, he turned the light off and walked out into the kitchen. He then went back into this bedroom, changed, and headed out the door.

When I knew he was gone I franticly pulled the blanket off; it was stifling under the blanket and bed. Another self-sabotage! That's when I knew my number was up and it was time to call an end to the missed school days! I had pushed this as far as I could take it and it was no longer time to play around.

I left for school and even though I was late, I still felt I needed to go in. When I got to class one of my teachers brought up the fact that, I had missed so many days and said, "You were doing so well before, why are you ruining everything by missing so many days of class?" Don't ruin it. Do what you need to do to graduate and move on with life." I didn't want to keep sabotaging myself at school.

I looked at her and took those words to heart; from now on I was not going to call myself out of class, no matter what.

Chapter Twenty-Four

As I was biking to school, I was crossing the street when I heard someone yelling out my name. It was kind of muffled at first because I had my headphones on and it wasn't until the honking started, that I looked over to see someone waving their arms in the air. I looked over to see who it was and of all people, it was Richard!

He was the guy from Loara High School who was heavy into drugs and good friends with the teacher's son who had committed suicide. I had neither seen nor talked to him in a long time and was wondering where he was going.

I walked over to his car and chatted with him for a bit and after a few minutes, I let him know I had to head to class. He also knew about the bullet situation and asked which school I got into and after telling him it was Gilbert East, he looked at me and said he was on his way over there too! I didn't really know what to say to him since it was a long while since we had talked. More importantly, with all the drugs he was taking, I wanted to stay far away from that crap. He took off and I continued on my way to class.

I was thinking how Richard ended up at this place and the only thing I could think of was, he got busted for drugs or something related to drugs. It was one or the other.

During lunch break I found Richard and asked him what happened. He explained how he was always getting high while at Loara. Every lunchtime he went out to his car and smoked before he went back to class. Often, when he went out to his car to get high, he came back to class, and someone would smell smoke all over him. He didn't get caught with any paraphernalia, but the fact he was high as a kite had gotten him expelled for drug use. Of course, it would be drugs. He then changed the conversation and asked how I was doing with my expulsion situation.

Ah, here we go with my situation. Word had spread all over Loara about what I had done in class that day. He said everyone knew and they were talking about it for a while. He even wanted to keep talking about it, but I looked at him and said, "I regretted every minute of what had happened. If I could take it all back, I would. But there was no way of turning back the clock and I had to deal with the consequences."

All he wanted to do was talk about the expulsion but the more I changed the conversation, the more he wanted details. Finally, the lunch bell rang, and we all headed back to class. That was our cue, and I was now done talking about the past.

Richard wanted to give me a ride back home so we could hang out for a little while. I had a feeling he would want to do something back at the house, but I didn't want to read too much into it, so I let it go and waited to see what was going to happen. My parents were not home, and I told him they were both at work until later on tonight.

We headed to the backyard and at that point, I knew exactly where this was going. He pulled out a couple of joints along with his lighter and started to light one up. I could see he was starting to get high as he blew the smoke straight up into the air. After smoking for a little bit, he grabbed a chair and asked if I wanted to try it.

At that point, I grabbed a chair grabbed and started to knock a few puffs back. It didn't take to long for me to feel the effects as time started to slow way down. After a couple hours of hanging out, Richard had to get going because he had to get to work. I looked at him and asked, "Dude, are you ok to drive? You look like your about to fall over." Just like anyone who is intoxicated would answer, he said, "Nah, I'm not high! I'm just feeling good, that's all." From that answer I knew he was stoned but he insisted on leaving.

I didn't say a word and as I closed the door, I went back out to the back yard to chill out for a while until my head cleared up. At this point I was foggy and my head spinning all over the place. I felt really relaxed and wanted to just hang out and do absolutely nothing. I was thinking the next time I saw Richard I would keep my distance. I was done. There was no excitement with what I was doing, so to me it didn't make sense to keep getting high.

I ran into Richard at school, and he asked me how I was feeling from yesterday. I told him I was feeling good, but I was done with smoking that stuff and wanted nothing more to do with it.

I was already dealing with drinking and the last thing I wanted to do was get addicted to weed. It was mostly because I did not want to get sidetracked and wanted to get the hell out of this place!

He respected my decision and would never offer it again.

Chapter Twenty-Five

Over the next couple of weeks, I was knocking off the list of requirements so I could finish school. I would even have side sessions with some of the teachers and ask them what I needed to do to get done faster. They were good and guided me along because they really wanted to see everyone graduate, even if some took longer than others. I never paid much attention to any of the other students there, but because as I was talking to some of the teachers on the side, some of the other students were taking notice.

Most of the time I was at school, I kept to myself because I did not want to get involved with what others were doing. I just wanted to get in and out as quickly as possible and move on. One day, I got quick notice of what a lot of the students really thought, since I was staying away from everyone. We had a fire drill and when the alarm went off, all the classes emptied out to the parking lot.

Each of the classes lined up in their separate areas to be accounted for, just like the usual fire drill in grade school. As we were all lined up outside in the parking lot, I squatted down on the ground and waited for the drill to get over with so I could go back inside. While all of the classes were outside, there was a lot of chatter going on.

After about fifteen minutes of waiting, the alarm was cancelled, and everyone went back into their classrooms. I went about my business as usual and got back to studying and went about my day.

During lunch time break, Richard ran over to me with a puzzled look on his face and told me he needed to tell me something. He was excited like he was holding back some breaking news. I looked at him and asked what was up? He said we needed to talk so we popped inside one of the classrooms away from everyone and when we were alone, he looked at me and blurted out, "Dude, the entire school thinks you are a nark!"

All I could do was laugh.

He shouted the same thing again and I continued to laugh my ass off as I could not believe what I was hearing! About everyone at the school thought I was a nark and I wondered if it was because I was staying away from everyone, or the fact I was talking to the teachers about getting my assignments done faster.

I couldn't stop laughing; it was the funniest thing I had ever heard! Me? A nark? After all of the stupid things I have done and why I ended up in this place!

I asked him where all of this coming from and he said it was all over the school and the word was out. I looked at him and told him straight out, "Dude, I could care less about what anyone here thinks about me. I don't care about any of their opinions or thoughts in any way, shape, or form because my goal was to get a high school diploma, and I am not interested in making any lifelong friends with any of them."

I guess to be in with the crowd you must be low on ambition and be a smoker, druggie, or drinker. If that meant I was not in with the crowd, perfect! These people are here for a reason and if they wanted to continue and stay here forever, that was up to them. I had other goals in life and staying here beyond my allotted time was not one of them.

After Richard told me about what they all said, he asked me what I was going to do. I looked at him and said absolutely nothing because I couldn't care less, and it wasn't worth my time. He was still standing and waiting for me to say something else so I finally told him everything was good, and he shouldn't worry about what others thought about me. I was totally fine with everyone thinking that because it did not faze me one bit.

He still didn't get it but when the bell rang, he walked off and I put all of what was said in the back of my mind and moved on from it quickly. My focus was on studying and getting done with these classes.

As class ended, I ran into Richard in the parking lot and was laughing when I saw him. He had asked me if I wanted a ride back home and I told him I was good, mostly because I didn't want him coming over to the house to smoke. After what had happened with the fire drill and being called a nark, I was seriously thinking about calling the Navy recruiter when I got home. I had been thinking about it off and on but now more so after everything I had learned today. I was more and more motivated to get this all done.

Joining the Navy was twofold; I would be out on my own, and I would have a job which would give me more real-world experience. Especially being a senior, I figured it was about time to see what I was going to be doing in the future.

Chapter Twenty-Six

Nineteen ninety - four seemed to be quickly passing by, and I made a promise to myself that I would get my diploma by the start of summer. More importantly, I was thinking about what I was going to be doing once I graduated. The one option that continued to play over and over in my mind was the Navy. What harm could it do to go and talk to a recruiter? So, one day I decided I was going to stop by the recruiter's office and see what he had to say.

The following day after class ended, I headed over to the recruiter's office with his business card in my pocket. When I parked my bike and headed in, I looked around the office and saw all kinds of cool retro Navy posters and recruiting material. Many of posters had captions saying, "See the World and Get a Great Education." It was all great to see but I still did not know if this was the right option for me. After all, I was not exactly on the right side of the page when it came to getting along with authority, especially taking orders from them.

Shortly after the recruiter finished up and came out of his office, I sat down and started to talk to him about how he stopped by the house and gave me his card. I also mentioned Jason's name and that he had just had my brother enlist in the Navy.

He asked me, "How Jason was doing?" I told him, "He was doing well, especially now that he was stationed down in San Diego." He then went on to ask me some basic questions like, "How much longer before you were going to graduate?", "What type of options do you have once you graduate?", but most importantly, "What kind of career path do you want to head down?" I was about four months away from graduating and I expected to be done sometime around May.

This was a big first step for me because I still didn't know what my future was going to have in store for me. He asked, "Was there any specific job that you were looking into?" and I told him, "I didn't know, but I for sure knew I wanted to be out of the house and on my own!" I wanted to hear more about what the recruiter had to say, especially his opinion on particular jobs.

I didn't know it at the time, but when you ask any military recruiter about the glamourous life of being enlisted and about the different jobs in the Navy, they will all talk it up like it's the greatest thing since sliced bread! No matter what job you took, you were going to be a glorified something or another.

After all this was the military.

Well, some of the perks he went on to explain and even show me pictures of places he had been to were, "You will be living on a ship with others and have an opportunity to see the world!" He then went on to say, "You will be going to other countries and seeing things no one else would be able to, unless you were either already on active duty or you were wealthy enough to be able to afford traveling the world."

"Wait", I thought to myself. "I can see the world and visit all kinds of countries all while getting paid?" "No way!" I told him, "Why isn't everyone doing this?" I asked right afterwards. He had officially reeled me in! This was too good of an opportunity to pass up! By the time he finished his sales pitch, my eyes popped wide open.

I was in total bewilderment because here I was an eighteen-year-old about to graduate high school and I now had the opportunity to see the world with the added perk of having a great job? No way! I could not lose! It was the opportunity of a lifetime! I was all excited and I told him, "I am ready to sign up right then and there and leave first thing the next morning!" I felt like I was finally on track and ready to move forward! He asked me, "Is this something I am willing to commit to?" and I told him, "Yes, a thousand times over yes!" I was all in!

Before I even had a moment to process everything he was talking about, I reached across his desk, grabbed a pen, and said, "Where do I sign? Let's not waste any more time and get this going!"

My first steps were going to be, he explained, "You will be taking take the ASVAB test and do a military physical which would take a couple of weeks to complete." "Once that process was completed, you will be moving on to the next phase and be picking out your job from hundreds that the Navy was offering." Wow!" I said, "The Navy has hundreds of jobs for me to pick from?" "You could be anything you wanted to be!" he said with a smile on his face!

I let him know I was willing to get it all done and excited to get it all started. He then gave me another card which had the date he would be calling me so I could take the ASVAB test. Honestly, it didn't take much for the recruiter to get me to join, especially with the potential opportunities. I was so ready to graduate and get some type of career going. Especially getting out of my parents' house!

I was so excited when I left, I sprinted back home as fast as I possibly could! I felt like I had found my golden ticket with the Navy! Once I got back, I yelled out to my parents, "Guess what! I am going to be joining the Navy! I got my golden ticket to get my life started!"

I was so exhausted and out of breath from the sprinting, it took me a minute to realize I just sprinted all the way home and left my bike at the recruiter's office. I let my parents know I would be right back because I had to go all the way back and get my bike.

After all of the trouble I had put myself through, it would only make sense I would pick something which would actually straighten my life out. My dad asked, "When was all of this was going to happen?" and I told him, "I was going to be taking the ASVAB soon and the physical shortly after." He also asked me, "What are you going to do as far as a job when you get in?" I told him, "I was still up in the air." More so, "I was not really sure as yet but, the Navy had hundreds of jobs for me to choose from and I am sure I can find something."

My dad mentioned, "Why don't you choose to become a Navy cook." A cook? "Why the hell would I want to join the Navy just to be a cook?" I said. It wasn't something that I was really interested in since I never cared for cooking. I wanted an exciting job, like a helicopter gunner, or even a field medic, just like I had seen in so many war movies. Those were the glamorous jobs! He kept insisting over and over that I should become a cook and not consider the other jobs. He emphasized and said, "That skill set of being a cook could be transferred back into civilian life after you completed your military service."

It wasn't the most exciting job, more so, the job I was even looking forward to. But after a lengthy conversation, I listened to what he had to say, for once, and now all I had to do was get the ASVAB done and move forward with the physical.

My dad also suggested I take some R.O.P classes in the meantime, which would give me a better understanding of becoming a chef. But there was another reason he suggested R.O.P and cooking in the Navy. He was also thinking of getting out of the theater production industry and doing something different like opening a restaurant and becoming a chef himself.

Since Jason was gone and I was about to be on my way out, all that would be left was my mom and younger brother, Jamie, who at the time was about three years old. My dad also figured this would be the perfect opportunity for him to look into changing his career path because he always loved cooking and would look into taking cooking classes with me.

The only thing left for me to do was figure out what I was going to be doing with the SlicTrack. It was a really great job and I liked how it was progressing, but I knew sooner or later I had to drop the news to Jackson that I was about to embark on another option once I graduated. If I was going to be taking the R.O.P classes after school and at the weekends, there was no way

I was going to be able to work at the track and take all these classes at the same time. I figured, though, once I had taken the ASVAB and got my score, it would give me a better idea about how soon I could be headed out to basic training

Chapter Twenty-Seven

I got a call from the recruiter asking if I was ready to take the ASVAB test. I hadn't done any studying and was going into the test cold. I just wanted to get the test out of the way and score as high as possible. He mentioned he would stop by to pick me up around 6 a.m. and would have some others who were also trying to get into the service.

6 a.m.? Who gets up that early? I headed to bed early that night to make sure I was able to get up in the morning. Shortly around 5:30 a.m., I heard a honk and it was the recruiter signaling for me to come outside. It was too early for me to get up, but I pushed through the early morning and packed myself in the van, anxious to get the test over with.

There was one girl, who was sitting in a seat frantically looking over the pretest. She looked nervous and I asked her if everything was all right. She said she was anxious about the test because she had already taken it a couple of times, and this was now her third try.

I asked if the test was really that hard and she said it was for her, but it doesn't mean it was for everyone else. She said the reason she was so anxious was because after taking the test twice and failing, if she failed it again today, she would have to wait another six months to take it all over again!

Wow! Six months is a long time to have to wait. All I could do was smile because I could not muster up any words after she said six months to wait for another retake. I turned my attention back to the drive, trying to think about something else instead of the test. I just wanted to make this a onetime exam and not have to worry about coming back and doing this all over again.

When we pulled up to the office, we got out of the van and walked in one at a time to look for our designated spots to take the test. I saw my recruiter and let him know I was ready to take the test. He asked me how much studying I had done leading up to exam day and I told him I never looked at any of the material. I was coming in from this point on with either I know it or I don't. He gave me a puzzled look because he wasn't sure how good I was going to do.

All that mattered to me at this point was to get the highest score possible then look at what career options were available. He then guided me to a room, sat me down and explained what was going to be on the test. He gave me some advice on getting a high score and told me to just relax. He asked one more time if I was ready and I told him, "A hundred percent yes, let's just get it done."

He left the room, and the clock was now ticking.

My heart was pumping and my eyes and brain were all dialed in because I was so excited to be able to finally move forward! This was one of those positive moments in life and I wanted to stop falling down the rabbit hole!

I started to go through the exam and knock out each section one by one. I was really digging into the material and trying to get it done as quickly as possible. Personally, I think being at Gilbert helped me with a lot of the material and it was the same type of testing, being self-paced. After about an hour I completed the test and turned in the study material. I asked them how long before it was to be graded. They said to go out and wait in the lobby with everyone else until they called out my name with the results.

We were all waiting anxiously to see how we each scored and just about everyone kept to themselves. No one wanted to deal with any of the stress we were all feeling. It was all pins and needles, sitting in the waiting area, when suddenly it came time for us to get our scores.

They were calling out everyone's name in alphabetical order and when it finally came time for my name to be called, I grabbed my packet and staring at me on the front page was a number 40. I kept staring at the number 40. What does this number 40 mean? Was it a good or a bad number? I kind of freaked out because I didn't know what the score meant.

When everyone received their packets, we all sat down with the training personnel so they could explain the scoring system. The minimum score you needed to qualify for the Navy was a 32, and if you didn't get at least the minimum score, you had to retake the test at another time. I blew out a big sigh of relief! A 32 just to get into the Navy and I got a 40! That was great news! I had made the enlistment cut, which was not bad for taking it the first time and putting in absolutely no study time whatsoever.

After getting my score, I went over to staff personnel and asked her if I was able to get the cooking job. She looked into her books and found the cooking job and replied I had made the cut for getting the training to become a cook. I looked at her and wanted to give her a big hug, but I didn't want to press it because I was worried there was some type of regulation about hugging an active military person.

Instead, I got up, shook her hand, and walked back to where I was sitting, grinning from ear to ear. It was a great feeling! I felt like I was walking on air and nothing could bring me down! I passed the test and qualified for the job all in the same day! When everyone else finished up with getting their results, we all waited for our rides to come pick us up and take us back to our recruiting stations.

As we all piled back into the vans, I saw the girl I was talking to on the way up and she wasn't looking so happy. I didn't know what to say because I didn't want to say something which would upset her since she looked as though she didn't pass the test again. I decided to at least see how she was doing and asked how she did on the test. I could see tears welling up in her eyes.

She said, "I scored a fifteen." I couldn't get any words out except it must have been a mistake especially since it was a thirty just get into the Navy. She said, "It was no mistake and I now had to wait another six months to take it all over again." I had to come up with something to say because of how bad she was feeling. I lied to her and said, "You shouldn't feel too bad because I didn't make it either. I was a couple points off from making the cut."

She said, "Really?" It was hard but I didn't want her to keep feeling bad and I told her that I would be back to retake the test. Hopefully, next time around she will get into the Navy. She looked at me and smiled back and said, "Thanks for all your support."

I knew I would never see her again and didn't see the harm in making up the story. After all, she felt better after hearing my results, so I guess it worked out pretty well.

We proceeded to talk about random stuff until we got back to the office. Once we all piled back out, I said my goodbyes and told her I would see her again sometime down the line. She got back into the van and that was the last time I ever saw her.

I walked into the recruiter's office and saw that he was waiting for the good news! He asked, "How did you do on the test?" I told him, "I made it in!" and "I scored high enough to get the cooking job I was aiming for!" He gave me a high five and yelled out, "YEA! CONGRATS!" I was so relieved because the first step was completed, and I was now moving on to take my physical.

He mentioned the next process and said, "Your physical is going to be an all-day event and I will be in touch with the date and time so be prepared for a very long day." We then proceeded to head back to the van and as the day was wrapping up, I felt like I accomplished everything I had set out for, which was great news!

When I got back home, I told my parents the great news! I said, "I scored high enough on the ASVAB and I had locked in the cooking job!" Now I had a hard confirmation of being accepted into the Navy and could see the light at the end of the tunnel. I was now officially a Navy recruit!

More importantly, I now had a concrete direction with the Navy. I knew I had to talk to Jackson about my job.

It was only going to be a matter of time before I left, and I wanted to give him a heads up about my plans. I figured once I got to work, I would give him all the details and turn in my two week notice.

Chapter Twenty-Eight

On Saturday, I arrived at work early so I could talk with Jackson. I explained to him I had just taken my entrance exam and was now a recruit for the Navy. More so, I was now in the process of getting my physical exams done, along with finalizing my background checks. He was kind of shocked at first because he had just hired me on for more hours. I told him I would be keeping the job as long as possible, until I had everything in line and my contract was signed.

Once I was all wrapped up with processing, I was going to put in my two week notice. He said it sounded like a great opportunity and wished me luck.

Just before I went to work, Jackson pulled everyone aside and gave an announcement. My decision had come at the most opportune time because when Jackson started to talk, he announced that within the next couple of months the track was going to shut down. The owner was about to sell the track to the city of Anaheim because they were in talks of expanding the freeway! Soon everyone would be out of a job. Now more than ever, I was glad I was enlisting!

Once word started to spread about the closure, everyone was taking the job a lot less seriously and goofing off more than usual. We all figured that since the track was shutting down, why not have as much fun as possible before we all went our separate ways?

So, we all started to really tune up the cars and make them go faster after the workday was done. It would be only a matter of time before the track was shut down and we all wanted to make the most of the time.

In the meantime, I would be in and out of the recruiting station getting my physicals and going through my background checks. While I was sitting at one of the desks, I was thinking back on how lucky I was not to have anything attached to my record! Especially with all the stupid crap I had done! It amazed me how fortunate I was not to have all those incidents turn into something more serious. More importantly, I didn't have a criminal record! I wanted to move past it all and start over fresh once I entered the military.

When my final background checks were completed and everything came up positive, my recruiter gave me the green light and I would be getting my first swear in when we finished up our last bit of paperwork! I could not believe I was about to finish up my processing! Once I did, I now belonged to the government and there was no turning back. All I had to do now was wait until I graduate from high school and afterwards, I would be getting my date for basic training!

Processing was now complete; I was told to get up and go into the main room where an officer was about to swear in about thirty others from all other branches. I lined up next to one of the others and when the officer said to raise your hand, we all at the same time recited the oath. Afterwards I was smiling ear to ear!

While we were wrapping up, we were told repeatedly to ***stay out of trouble*** because if we went out and did something stupid, the consequences would be more severe. Moreover, we would be charged by the civilian and the military side of punishment. ***Stay out of trouble***, were the key words.

If I were to take away anything form my learning experience, it was to stay out of trouble. Those words just flowed off of my lips like water flowing down a slow rushing river, *stay out of trouble!*

Now that we were all wrapped up, we grabbed our packets and headed back to our vans. Once again, we headed back to our respective drop off points and my recruiter was waiting for me. I gave him all the details and I had a ship out date of around December to leave for basic training. This would give me enough time to graduate and have everything in line before I headed out to Great Lakes, Illinois. All my focus was to graduate and get a copy of my diploma over to him. When I left his office and headed back home, I kept telling myself, repeatedly, to ***stay out of trouble*** because I now belonged to the Navy.

As one last measure, if I were to get into trouble, I had to let my recruiter know right away as he had to be the first to know. If something were to happen…

Chapter Twenty-Nine

Now that I had my schedule, I could now focus on what was ahead of me. My dad, in the meantime, had found some R.O.P classes and signed us both up. I was a bit excited because I was going to be focusing on becoming a cook! I figured; it was something different to do in the meantime while waiting to head out to Boot Camp.

Once I was all set up with the R.O.P classes, I went to work over the weekend and told Jackson I was giving him my notice. He was incredibly supportive of my decision, and I could also see that he was getting less interested in the track since it was closing down. Even the operators did not care what was happening on the track as everyone was smashing their cars into each other and creating havoc.

At one point, several of the employees began to take the cars off the track and started to race them down the side streets!

All of this would carry on over the next two weeks and when my day had finally come to check out, it was an extremely hard moment for me because of all of the life lessons and experiences at this job. I talked to Donald and he let me know he was still going to be working over at the chicken house and if I ever had an opportunity to stop by I should. I let him know I would see him again sometime down the line, which by chance I would many years later.

I headed out the gates thinking about all of the fun I had, and I knew everything was going to work out for Donald; he always had that great positive attitude. It was a great time and one I will never forget.

Once I left, I would never see the track again because the street would be part of the new freeway which was being built right were the track stood.

Another lesson I learned from working there was you can never get in the way of progress; life is always going to continue no matter what happens. When one door closes another one opens and for the track it meant progress was going to be better for everyone.

My focus had now shifted away from the track and into the R.O.P classes and when they started up, I could already tell this was going to be a long couple of months. All of the running back and forth from school and R.O.P. made the days drag out to what felt like a 30 hour daytime frame.

On the first day of class, my dad and I both went up together so we could get any paperwork filled in and get a basic understanding on how the classes were going to go. When the head chef came out and introduced himself, he talked for a little bit and then started to give out assignments to everyone and put us in specific areas suited to how much knowledge we already had.

He told my dad he would start him in the kitchen along with the other chefs because he had some experience. I had no experience whatsoever and would be starting at the very bottom. He wanted me to start by understanding the menu and waiting on tables. Part of the overall curriculum was learning everything about the business from the ground up and it started for me in the front of the house, being a waiter.

We jumped right into the program, and I absorbed the menu, quickly getting into a rhythm. I was taking the orders from the customers and when I went into the kitchen giving the chef the ticket, I would observe the kitchen, how it operated and how the plates looked when they came out to the table. I was now starting to understand the basic steps when each plate was prepared.

It finally clicked in why the head chef started me out as a waiter and his process. As the day moved on, we finished up the class and I felt like I had gained some good experience. We now had our working orders and moving forward I would absorb everything the class had to offer.

It was an exhausting period of time, but I liked the fact I was learning as much as I possibly could about the food service industry. The long days also meant that I was going to be needing a lot of energy and I needed to get down as much information as possible. Every time I went into the kitchen, I pounded down as much food as I could put inside me. Not only were these the right classes I needed but, more important than anything else, I was staying away from trouble. For the time being…

Over the next two months, I learned everything I could by taking on all of the responsibilities in the front of the house. There was nothing else for me to learn, which meant I finally worked my way into the kitchen and was now able to learn the back side of the house. I was excited to get started because this was where I wanted to be!

It felt good once I was assigned to work with a chef, trying to absorb and learn as much information as possible. I would work with my dad here and there but, I would be under a chef who has been at the program and had more kitchen experience.

While working with the program chef, I was eating and tasting everything, I could get my hands on, just so I could understand how all of the ingredients went together. I was learning a lot, but I also knew my time with the R.O.P. classes was coming to an end since it would be closed over the summer. This also meant I had to finish school the same time R.O.P let out because of my deadline.

Once the program was all wrapped up, my focus shifted back to completing school. What I really needed was a way to speed up the process. I was getting anxious with how few classes I had left. There weren't that many but, enough to keep my mind turning.

Remember back when I talked about figuring out a way to work the system in getting done with my classes a lot sooner? I had figured out a way and formulated a gamelan!

In one of my classes, I observed a teacher as he went over to a cabinet and pulled out some assignments for the week. I continued to watch where he was looking in the cabinet and pulling out more schoolwork for us to do. I figured the tests, quizzes, and answer keys were also stashed inside the cabinet! I was also observing another student who was just as anxious to get done with the class as I was.

After figuring out who I could work with on my plan, I let the student know what we would be doing. He would go over to the teacher and ask him a couple of questions. While they were talking, I would go over to the file cabinet and take a quick peek inside. Then I would move some papers around looking to find the class materials we needed. The system worked! Staring right in front of me were the tests and the answer keys! Jack pot! Not only did I have all the information on class assignments for the week but I also scored all the testing information for the exams!

Once I took it all in, I backed away from the cabinet and looked over at the other student to let him know I was done looking inside the cabinet. We both sat down and continued with our work until it was break time. When we had our lunch, we went outside, and I let him know what I found. We came up with a plan as to how we were going to get the answers for each of the sections for the schoolwork and the exams.

As class was going out for the day, we would take turns distracting the teacher while the other one would sneak into the file cabinet, pull out the answer keys, and write the answers down. When class began the next day, we already had all the information we needed to get our work done.

We were both taking a major risk. The excitement of getting caught was just enough to get my heart pounding, my body shake with anticipation and keep my focus dialed in! But was it worth the possibility of getting caught and getting expelled from Gilbert East? It sure as hell was! In the end I talked myself into thinking that this was the fastest way to complete the class. In the end, it did not faze me as much as I thought it would.

Instead of taking the proper amount of time, which was usually about four months, to complete the economics course, we wrapped it up in about six weeks. We achieved our goal and can now look ahead to the next class. We stepped out of the classroom and moved on to our next class together. Instantly I was scouting the teacher to see if he also kept his class assignments and exams in the same type of cabinet.

Fortunately for us, it was the same situation! We were both working in tandem, completing the next class at lightning speed. I was now more confident than ever that I was going to be able to graduate by the summertime.

Before I knew it, I was completing my last class! We had both knocked off several months and I was only one class away from graduating! The difference was I had completed them so fast, I was on a pace to get it all done by the end of spring instead of summer! My plan had worked masterfully!

This never would have happened without the help of the *study aids*. In reality, I cheated my way through the better part of my senior year. I just wanted to get school behind me and move forward. I knew I was missing out on a lot of learning, but at this point I was over all this crap!

Shortly thereafter, I was on my last exam, but before I started, I sat quietly for a couple of minutes just staring at the exam. Thinking back on everything I had put myself through over the last several years. Having all the highs and lows along with all the ups and downs, turning my world upside down. Reality was finally sinking in on how far I had come.

When the teacher put the test down in front of me, I collected my thoughts and went on as usual; I already knew the answers since I had read over the answer key. After about an hour, I circled my last answer, put my pencil down while having a big grin on my face. I knew I passed the exam and had to contain my emotions. I just wanted to get up, scream, jump, yell, that is how excited I was. I then got up from my desk, turned in the exam, shook the teacher's hand and headed out the door. I didn't want to run; I wanted to take it slow. I felt like I was on cloud nine.

I was finally done with high school and ready to close the book on this chapter of my life!

When I got back home, I sat down on the couch and just chilled out for a while, since I was still taking everything in and enjoying the moment. When my parents got home, I told them I had just taken my last exam and I was done with high school FOREVER!

My mom then asked me about graduation. I told her I did not know and would go up to the school tomorrow to find out. All I wanted to do for the rest of the day was absolutely nothing.

I went back to school the next morning and headed over to the principal's office. He explained that once it was all official, I would be getting a phone call from his office letting me know my diploma would be ready for me to pick up. It was a short conversation, so I grabbed my bike and headed back home waiting around for the phone to ring.

After a couple of days of waiting, the principal's office called, letting me know I could come down and pick up my diploma! I was smiling and excited all at the same time! I let them know I would be on my way shortly. My parents and younger brother all piled into the car, and we drove to the school.

I jumped out of the car and speed walked over to the office. Right inside the door was the principal holding my diploma in his hand. I didn't know what to say or do at first because I didn't know what to expect. I walked over and stood in front of him, he spoke some words like congratulations on getting your diploma, good luck in life, etc. etc. Smiling and looking around, I realized I was the only one standing in the office, and it finally dawned on me that I was the only one who was graduating today!

I started joking with him saying I was one in a class of one and I should give some type of speech to the graduating class. He also started to laugh because it was crazy to be standing by myself with a solo graduation.

He said some parting words and I thanked him again for allowing me to attend the school. He handed me my diploma and finally I was now officially a high school graduate! It was the best feeling in the world in finally being done will all of this! More so, what I had put myself through in ending up here in the first place.

While I was walking out, he asked me if I had any plans for the future. I told him I was now ready to ship out to basic training since I had my diploma. He gave me a good luck and all the best. I walked out and got into the car showing my parents the diploma.

On the way back home, I pulled out my diploma once again, just to gaze over it. This was one of the best pieces of paper I had ever set my eyes on! I also concluded I was not going to have a graduation party like Jason had; I wasn't going to have the gifts and the after party he had experienced.

Overall, I was fine with it because in the end, it really didn't matter all that much, especially with how I ended up getting my diploma anyway…

Chapter Thirty

Now that I was officially finished with school and had a December leave date for basic training, I had a nice block of time before I shipped out. My dad asked me what I was going to do for the time being, but I wasn't quite sure. He suggested I get a job so I could keep myself occupied and stay out of trouble.

For once I agreed with him, so I started looking around to see who was hiring. I wanted something that was seasonal in case I needed to leave at a moment's notice. I learned the amusement parks were always hiring, so I gave the Knott's Berry Farm employment office a call. Within a few minutes they suggested attractions and told me to come in for an interview in a couple of weeks.

Now all I needed to do was keep myself occupied until my interview. I had time to spare and with too much time came the possibility of trouble…

Out of the blue, I got a call from Binh, one of the guys from the group. I should have left well enough alone; I knew if I got back together with these particular guys, I was going to find myself doing something stupid. It had been a long time since we all had talked and I figured if I let them know I was going to be leaving for basic training in a few months, everything would be good.

We met for lunch during the week and spent a few hours catching up with each other. After we finished, Binh asked if there was somewhere we could talk for a while without anyone else listening in on the conversation. I told him I was staying over at my cousin's house for the time being and the house was going to be empty since my cousin was going to be out at work.

Just as we were about to leave, Binh had asked if a couple of the others from our group could also come over and I said, "Why not! It's been a while since I had seen the others." So, he made a couple of calls and I then gave them my address so we can all meet up at the same time.

After we all had met up at my cousins house, we all went inside, got some drinks, and began to catch up on life. It's been a long while since I had seen us all together and I was curious to see how everyone had been doing.

We spent a few hours having some drinks and chatting, when out of the blue, one of the guys in the group mentioned something about how they were making a lot of money and wanted to bring me in on the plans. "I knew they were involved in something!" I thought to myself. They were always looking for different routes or getting ideas on making extra cash on the side. Just like I had done so many times in the past. But this time around I wanted to stay on the side lines and not get involved. I had now said my vows to the Navy and needed to stay out of trouble for as long as possible!

Remember the words **"Stay out of trouble."**
"STAY…OUT…OF…TROUBLE!"

He had said the magic words, "Making some extra cash on the side" which were now playing inside my head over and over and over again! I needed to keep telling myself, "Stay the course! You don't want to waste what you have in front of you" and "Your so close to getting into the Navy! Don't ruin it!"

But my mind kept peeking its ugly head into the rabbit hole, just so it could see what the potential was in making some extra money on the side.

As quickly as I dropped into the rabbit hole saying, **NO! NO! NO!** I now had popped out to the other side saying, "What's the gameplan?" and "How much money can I be making from this adventure?" But the most important aspect out of all this was, I was going to be getting some major juice from this! I was going out with one last bang before basic training! This was exactly what I was looking for!

I knew I was going to regret my decision, but in the end, my need for excitement had won out and I was now on board!

Over the next several hours, Binh had gone into very fine details of what I was going to be doing and how I was going to be making a lot of cash. We went over a gameplan of driving schedules, for how long I was going to be on the road for as well as bank routes, in how many banks I was going to be able to stop into for the day. It was all about going from bank to bank on the shortest drive and visiting as many branch locations in as many grouped locations as possible before my time had run out.

This was awesome! Every hour that went by and the more I heard the plan, the more my heart was pounding with excitement! My hands were shaking just from hearing about all this! The sunlight inside the house was even beginning to mess with my eyes because I could sense that my pupils had been dilated to the max from all the anticipation!

We kept talking for a while longer and had a few more drinks. I could start to feel my body run itself down a bit from all of the constant excitement and could feel it process out the extra adrenaline I had produced from earlier.

My brain had been filled to the max with all of this new and wonderful information. More so, my body had overexerted itself and I was starting to fatigue. I couldn't keep my focus up so I told the guys I had hit my limit and we needed to call it a day. I showed them all to the door and we all agreed on a date and time when we will be off and running with our plan. But before we got into the first phase of the plan, there was something I had to do first.

My first order of business was to go down to the DMV and report my ID as stolen. I had to fill out some paperwork and put in a request to get a new license ordered right away. Once the DMV was taken care of, I would have to wait a few days just to make sure they were on top of getting my new ID paperwork processed.

Once I had the green light for getting my ID processed, we were all going to meet back up at my cousin's house and move onto the next phase of the plan. I was getting all squeamish and giddy from the anticipation!

When everyone arrived at my cousins house, we got some more drinks and were all gathered in one of the spare bedrooms so they could set up shop. One of the guys had brought a computer and laser printer with them and were now ready to show me what was going to be making us a lot of money!

They plugged in their computer and loaded a program onto the screen. They showed me an account on the screen that had a lot of money in it! It was in the low millions but to me, it was a small fortune staring me in the face! I got the run down on what the account was being used for. They had someone on the inside of a corporation who had set up a fake profile and were able to hack inside the accounts. The inside person was to get one of the corporate account numbers so it could be reprinted on a different paycheck. We were now going to be using that information for our personal use and creating a check that was using the stolen corporate account number.

We simply got all of the required check information for the corporate account and were about to make all of the funds disappear. In essence, it was a stolen corporate account, made into a fake corporate check, that was about to be bled dry in the matter of a few days! Now that there programs were all set up and ready to go, I saw the printer light up and heard it being calibrated so it could start printing.

At first, I looked over at the printer as it was getting ready to print and thought that this was crazy. I mean they had the account numbers and the information on the corporate accounts, but how were we going to be making money from this information? They were talking over and over about printing checks but even I knew that it was easy to see how a fake check could be spotted if you held it up to the light. Even the feel of the paper was different compared to a regular piece of paper from a printer, compared to the paper used for a paycheck.

Once the printer was all warmed up, Binh began loading up some paper and hitting the print button. I took a peek at the type of paper that was being loaded, just to see what it looked like. To my surprise, the paper that was being loaded was all folded into squares, with perforations and it even had a darker color to it. I told myself, "There was no way these pages were going to pass as an actual check." Once a page came out of the printer, Binh handed a page to one of the guys so they could start tearing along the perforated lines. I just watched as the tearing continued one after another and were then stacked up in a pile. Once the last page went through the tearing and was stacked up, it was no time to inspect the work.

I picked one up in my hand and couldn't believe it! The piece of paper in my hand looked and felt like an actual paycheck! I asked Binh how this was possible and he said, "Not only did we get the corporate account number, we also got the paper that the checks were printed off of."

"Holy Hell!" I shouted, "The actual paper that the corporation uses to print off the paychecks and pay its employees!" "That paper?" I said. Reality had finally sunk in. They had actually done the impossible. Each check that was printed was a ticket to get paid! I could see and feel how these checks looked identical to a regular paycheck!

Now that all the checks were cut, printed and ready to go, we moved onto the next phase of our plan. Our objective was to cash as many of the checks as quickly as possible before time expired. The checks had an extremely limited shelf life and needed to be deposited into the bank before the accounting department caught on to their funds being cleaned out. Once time had expired, it meant the corporation had caught on and the account was terminated and all checks going forward were no longer valid to be cashed.

I stood for a moment thinking to myself, if this was just one account that we were working on, how many other accounts were there? For that matter, how many accounts were already bilked for their money? I was curious to see so I asked Binh, "How many accounts were you guys and others working on?" He told me not to think about it but did say, "We and some others outside of us have a network that was constantly changing itself up with the account numbers and bilking the accounts for a lot of money." "Well then" I said to myself. Apparently there was quite a few people who were in on this. The whole purpose was to make as much money as they possibly could from the corporations before they had been shut down and moved onto the next one. We continued on for a few more hours with drinking and going over some more details.

After a while we decided to call it a day. I was officially out of energy and couldn't think straight anymore.

On the way out, Binh went on to explain why I did what I did with my ID card. It dawned on me it was a protective measure in that if I went to the DMV and reported my ID as stolen and something had happened, I would not be in trouble because my ID would show up in the system as stolen. It had given me limited liability in case anything had gone wrong, or so I thought…

Before I closed the door, Binh asked, "When will you be willing to start?" I said, "The sooner the better because I was ready to cash as many of these as I possibly could before I left for basic training." We both smiled and laughed because we knew it was all about the money and we wanted to get as much as we possibly could.

He said one final thing before he let in that, "I will have a driver come pick you up in the morning and be ready for a long day." Everything was set and ready to go. I sat down on the couch thinking about tomorrow with how much money I was going to be making.

At this point, I needed to keep myself calm and not over think things too much. After all, tomorrow was going to be a day full of fun and excitement!

Chapter Thirty-One

I was super excited and pumped for the day as I could already feel my heart, beat like a drum and all of my senses started to dial themselves in. Once I heard a honk, I looked out the front window to see who it was. A white truck was waiting for me, and I told my parents I would be out for the day. I flew out the door to the waiting truck and we jumped on the freeway heading towards San Diego.

We discussed our game plan and went over some basic precautions. My driver, Dom, then gave me some checks, each in the amount of four hundred and seventy-two dollars even. I asked Dom why the checks were that specific dollar amount and he said it was because any check written over the amount of five hundred dollars had to be called in by the bank for verification, since it was considered a *red flag*. It made total sense; we wanted to get in and out of the banks without arousing any suspicion.

Another activity to watch out for was whether the teller entered numbers on the computer screen to verify the check, or if the manager was asked to approve anything. In that case, I was supposed to immediately walk out the front door and not look back. Apparently, this was a sign that account was compromised, definitely a red flag. He repeatedly stressed that I should get out if the bank manager became involved.

I was taking mental notes of all this: I wanted everything to go as smoothly as possible. More so, I was getting myself dialed in to keep my focus once I walked inside the bank. I was also feeling some anxiety about what I was about to do, but I was getting all fired up!

We approached our first stop and as I stepped out of the truck, my body surged with excitement! My palms were sweaty, my body was shaking with anticipation and I could hear a pin drop! I was all nice and dialed in and headed towards the door, all the while looking around at every square inch of the bank branch, the customers, observing the staff inside the building, and constantly peeking out at the parking lot, looking at every little detail.

While I was in line waiting for my turn, I looked for the youngest tellers since they most likely had less experience and were probably not as observant as the other tellers. I walked up to the teller's window and started to make small talk. I pulled out the check and asked if it was all right for me to cash my paycheck here. She took the check and asked for my ID so I went into my pocket, took it out and handed it to her along with the check.

We continued with the small talk while she looked up my information on the computer. My heart was racing a mile a minute and felt like it was going to rip right out of my chest. I was so consumed with excitement! Every vein in my body was pumping with so much blood, I could see them coursing through my skin. I was even starting to tremble a bit! I just tried to keep my mind on the task at hand. With every second that went by, I was craving more and more of this awesome feeling!

After a minute or two of small talk, she looked over at me and asked me how I wanted the bills. I finally got the words out of my mouth and replied that I would like the bills in twenties. She went into her cash drawer and pulled out the money and set it on the countertop while counting it out. I looked at every single bill she put down and heard the cash register ring with every count.

When she finished, she asked me if there was anything else she could do for me. I quickly replied everything was good and scooped up the cash and put it in my pocket. I walked out the front doors with a huge grin on my face knowing I was off to a great start!

I was trying to calm myself down and didn't want to get carried away by the experience. I began to take some deep breaths and eventually relaxed a little. Dom had seen me walking and swung around to pick me up. He asked me how everything had gone down, and I gave him a thumbs up!

Next up was another bank and I got nice and pumped up, walked inside, and went about business as usual. I got the cash from the check and headed back out, the same basic routine.

This was going great! We were both making lots of cash and having a good time. Our escapade went on for hours and hours and sometime around late afternoon, we were getting to the point where we needed to eat. We tried to find the best and most expensive place we possible could because after all, we were already sitting on several thousand dollars and felt like we could afford a very nice meal.

We drove around for a little bit until we found a nice seafood place, so we pulled over and went inside. When we sat down, we looked at the menus and scoped out the most expensive item we could possibly find. Our waiter let us know the fish was set at a higher price compared to the rest of the menu, but we let him know we didn't care.

After we ordered, we talked a little bit more about our plan and the bank branches on our route. We took out some maps and drew out our route, marking the branches so we could find them as quickly as possible.

Dom asked me how I was feeling, and I let him know I was ready for more!

When our food arrived, we pretty much inhaled it, not wanting to waste any more time. Shortly after, we headed back on the road and over the next couple of hours, I was banging out check after check and stockpiling the cash inside the truck. After a while, we decided to call it a day. We were both exhausted from all the driving and my enthusiasm was winding down.

As we got back to our home area, we went into another expensive restaurant and spent a little bit more money but now it was payday time! We ate as quickly as we could and once we finished, we went into the bathroom, locked the door, and counted all of the bills. My eyes popped wide open because when he pulled all the cash out of his pocket, there were stacks of twenties and fifties.

Dom continued to count all the cash, he was handing over a lot of the money, and I couldn't count it fast enough! He was giving me hands full of cash at a time and when we finished all the counting, I had several thousand dollars cash in my hand! I just stood silently for a couple of minutes trying to comprehend all that we had accomplished for the day. I had never seen so much money in my entire life! It was such a rush!

After we counted it all out, we headed back to the car. I still couldn't contain my excitement because after all how could I? It was a crazy day, and everything had gone according to plan. Dom asked me if I was up for another round on another day and I took a couple of seconds to think about. I couldn't say no because I was having way too much fun. He then mentioned he would be back in contact and figure out another day for another run.

As I walked into the house and unloaded all of the cash onto my bed, I stacked it all up nicely, but now I had to find a place to stash it. I left it all in my dresser drawer, for the time being, until I could find another place for it. My mind was spinning a mile a minute, anticipating what I wanted to buy with all of this cash. But it really didn't matter to me what I did with the cash; it was dirty money after all.

Throughout the night I would start to contemplate my wish list, since the money was burning a huge hole in my pocket. All I could hear was spend, spend, spend! I tried to keep my thoughts under control - I needed to get to sleep so I could have the energy for tomorrow. After all, I wanted to cash out at least another twenty checks and build up my stockpile in the dresser drawer and buy even more stuff.

Over the next couple of days, I waited around until I got a phone call from Dom letting me know he was on the way over. I was ready and excited! In what had seemed like forever, I heard him honk and I grabbed a couple of things. I jumped in the passenger seat and asked what the game plan was.

This time around we were going to start up in Los Angeles and work our way back down to Orange County. We headed on to the freeway and started our way up towards L.A. and arrived at our first destination. Keeping to my same routine as before, I walked into the bank, got up to the counter, and went about my business as usual. I picked up the bills, smiled at the teller and walked out the door. I jumped into the truck, and we headed to the next bank.

After knocking several of them off the list, we pulled up to our next one, but this time around, I did not scout out the area. I think I was getting a false since of security because everything was going so smoothly, I started to let my guard down a bit and became more relaxed. This had now become so routine that the sense of excitement had now disappeared.

Cashing the checks had become way too easy. I would just walk in, get the cash, and I had no worries about getting caught. Don't get me wrong, getting all of this money was a blast because, after all, who was I to complain about making close to twelve thousand dollars in about two days? My most difficult task was going into a bank and cashing a fake check! But part of the reason for doing all of this was for an exciting day and if it was no longer exciting, what was the point of continuing?

Knocking out bank after bank, I needed a break. As usual, we found the most expensive place to eat. Our waiter came over and took our order and once he walked away, we went back to business and plotted out the rest of our routine. Like last time, Dom looked at me and asked if I wanted to keep it going or call it a day. I let him know I was still in a groove and wanted to keep it going. Right after I said those words, I had this gnawing suspicion.

Deep down, I knew my luck was bound to run out, especially with my concentration becoming almost nonexistent. It goes back to when I was stealing toys at Gemco and got busted by the store security officer. From that instance, I learned I needed to be more observant with my surroundings and make sure I was in total control of the situation. But there are times when you, "Hope for the best and plan for the worst" and still come out with a negative outcome.

In essence, getting caught red handed!

In my head it was only a matter of time before the account had been found out by the corporation and was shut down. This was why I wanted to push this as far as I could and get as many of these checks cashed as quickly as possible!

So, we ate as fast as we could, had our banks plotted out and paid for lunch. We headed out the door and set off to another bank.

It was one success after another and I was feeling good, but I also knew I was pressing my luck with every passing moment. Number 14 was now up, and I was officially ***not*** keeping up with my protocols and this particular bank was the one which turned the tide.

As usual, my process started off as it normally did. I got dropped off in the parking lot at a different location every time, just so we did not create the same patterns at each branch. Once I was dropped off, I would scout out the parking lot as well as the front of the branch just to see if there were security guards. If there were, I needed to know how many of them were located in the parking lot and in front of the branch. I also wanted to know the quickest escape route if something were to happen and get out of the area as quickly as possible.

When I approached the branch and walked inside, I quickly looked around to see how many cameras were and where they were located. I knew they would be recording the entire process but, I would at least get an idea of how they would be recording my transaction.

I also wanted to know if the branch tellers had an open area or if it was covered in bullet proof casings. I figured, if the teller didn't have any bullet proof casings walled off in front of them that they would be more cordial and will make cashing the check an easier transition.

Once I found out how the teller was operating, I would then proceed to scout out each of the tellers personalities. I looked for traits such as: age, attire, mannerisms, and the most important attribute was attitude. I was looking for a young teller, neatly dressed, with a loose fitting personality. Once I matched those attributes to my chosen teller, I was now ready to make my transaction.

I had found my teller of choice and went about business as usual, ignoring all of the protocols I had put together. Internally I was supposed to be keeping up with all of my protocols, but with every success, came complacency. It had all come to me too easily with cashing all of the checks. Now I was not listening to my gut feeling or for that matter, ignoring all safety measures inside my head.

I went up to the counter, approached the teller and gave her my check. I made some idle chit chat to break the ice and keep the conversation in my favor. She mentioned that I had not signed the back side. Once I did, I gave it back to her, and she took it from me and said she needed to verify some information. The whole process was moving along nicely, just as it had the other 13 times before.

Until she started typing on her keyboard…

This time around, the process was taking a bit longer than normal while she was typing in the account number on the check. With every passing click of a key, my heart started to pound like crazy! Thoughts of, "Was the account closed down?" "Was the whole operation now in jeopardy?" danced around inside my head. I knew I needed to keep myself calm, even though my body was shaking and I could feel sweat dripping down my back! All I could do at that point was look at her and keep my mind on the moment. Most importantly, I told myself, "Don't Panic!!!"

While she was looking at the computer screen and pulling down the check information, I looked over at her face and could instantly tell there was something wrong. Her eyes were starting to squint and dart back and forth at the screen. She then changed her facial expression as if she had a look of concern on it! The seconds ticked away and I was now starting to plan my exit route. I needed to leave before she did something drastic!

She looked up from her computer screen and said, "Everything was good with the check, but needed to go see the manager to verify something." She was the first teller to ever do this and it was freaking me out! "So much for my personality traits protocol!" I thought.

Once she picked up the check, closed her computer screen and walked back to see the manager, instantly my heart started to pound a mile a minute and thousands of thoughts were ripping through my brain! I kept thinking, should I stay while she verifies my information, or should I walk out of the bank and call it quits? What if she was going back to call the police? All I could do was stand there and wait until the branch manager verified my information because I did not want to chance making a scene.

When they both finally came over, the branch manager introduced himself, I stared back and calmly smiled because I didn't want to arouse anymore suspicion. They both started to talk to each other to make sure the check was on the up and up. I listened in while standing in my same spot smiling. It was not until a couple of minutes later that they both ran the background check on me and when they finished looking everything over, words were starting to come out of their mouths. This was it! I was now planning for the worst because I had been caught in the act! I squinted my eyes a tiny bit waiting to get busted and then all of a sudden, I heard the question, "How would you like your bills?"

How would I like my bills she asked! No, "Holy Crap!" button this time! From that point on I let out a small sigh of relief and instantly wiped that stupid grin off my face. I was still trying to stay calm throughout the whole ordeal taking small, deep breaths. I barely got out the words, *any denomination works for me*. She then reached into her drawer, pulled out some bills and counted them in front of me. Right after, she asked me if there was anything else I needed. I mustered up what smile I could and told her everything was good. I then picked up the cash and headed out the door.

I felt as if I was carrying a heavy load from all of the overloaded anxiety pushing throughout my body. It was making me shake more than usual because of the fear factor I had just experienced.

Eventually I headed over to the truck and jumped in. Dom immediately knew I was a bit frazzled because of the look I had on my face and the sweat which was dripping down. He looked at me and was a little shocked, while asking if everything was all right? Was there any trouble with the bank? I told him I had a bit of a close call, but the end result turned out to be a good. He then asked if I wanted to continue with the routine.

I knew right then and there I should stop the madness and call it a day. This was a close call, and I was lucky to walk out without any problems. My time was running out of seconds and this all needed to stop. In the end, I couldn't do it. Physically the need to keep pushing forward was consuming me. With the thought of almost getting caught, my protocols were back on! I was at the point of no return, and I knew I couldn't stop any of this; I wanted to keep it going until every last check was cashed.

Especially after my close call, the rush was back making me feel all too good and I wanted more.

Despite what had just happened, I looked over at Dom and told him to press on. I think even he knew that we should have stopped, and he was a bit reluctant to go on. I looked over at him, asked him where the next bank was, and I let him know I was ok to move forward. But right before we pulled out of the driveway, he asked me one more time if I was good to continue on. I think he just wanted to check and see if I still had the energy to continue but at that moment I should have asked him what he thought.

If he would have hesitated with only the slightest conviction, I would have called it a day and left well enough alone. Since he left it up to me and didn't saying, I felt like I needed to get the job done and finish out what he had started.

So, we buckled up, left the parking lot, and headed out in search of our next bank.

This is when it all fell apart…

Chapter Thirty-Two

While Dom was driving, I tried not to think about the close call that was still lingering in my mind. It wasn't so much as a close call per se, but a call close enough as to wake me up and think about what I was doing. "Anything could have happened" I thought with that last teller. I definitely needed to step up my game and keep myself in the moment.

More so, I really needed to focus on my exit strategy and be prepared. I didn't want to think about it but what if something were to happen in my next transaction? "Was I going to be able to make it out of the branch without being caught?" I thought to myself. This is where I needed to plan ahead and continue to stick with my protocols

After some thinking and calming myself down, eventually I got back to a normal state of mind. I collected my thoughts and was now focused on the task at hand.

We kept driving until we arrived at the next bank, but before I left the truck, Dom asked me once again, "Are you ready for another bank, or do you want to call it a day?" He said, "There's nothing wrong with calling it since we already made a lot of money" I looked at him and said, "I am good to go! This one would be lucky number 15 and I will stop once this last one is cashed out."

My near miss had put me back on point and when I stepped inside the bank, it was back to business as usual. I noticed the tellers here appeared to be more mature, meaning they were in there mid to late forties. Taking that into consideration, I hopped in line and waited for my turn to be called.

When I approached the teller, my mind kept turning because she was not like the others. Internally I could feel something was off, but my adrenaline had gotten the better of me. I approached the teller and handed her my check. After I signed it and handed it over, she pulled up the computer screen and started typing on the keyboard. She was not showing any kind of emotion, making it very hard to get a read.

All I could do was stand and wait, wondering if it was a green light or not.

After a couple of seconds, she asked for my ID so she could verify my information. Without saying a word, I handed over my ID and she started to type my information on the computer screen. After she finished typing on the computer, she picked up the check and my ID then turned to me and said she needed to take the check back to her manager to verify the information and I needed to wait at the window until she got back.

Oh crap! I knew exactly where this was going! Ding, Ding, Ding! I was now officially out of time! I let her know I would wait until she returned. But of course, I was not going to stick around! I needed to walk slowly out of the bank and not look back. As soon as she was out of sight, I turned around and headed to the front door, walking out calmly so as to not make a scene.

As I reached the front door, I scouted out the truck and walked around a little bit to not to give up on the driver. I made eye contact with him and walked all the way to the end of the parking lot. I turned around to peek at the bank door and I saw the teller looking around the parking lot with the check in her hand. She was frantically looking all over while calling for security.

When Dom saw the look on my face, he stayed put for a couple of minutes to not arouse any suspicion. He pulled up and I just about crawled inside because I wanted to keep a low profile. Once inside, I explained everything. Lucky number 15 was officially my last check, and the bank now had my ID!

We sat in the truck for a few minutes waiting for the perfect time to drive off. After we saw the teller and the manager go back inside the bank, we started the truck up and took off slowly. I was sitting as far back in the seat as I could so no one could see my face. Once we got onto the freeway, Dom asked me what happened.

I went over every detail letting him know they had taken my ID along with the check. He kept telling me everything would be ok if I stuck with the plan. I was not hearing anything he was saying because all I could think about was what was I going to tell my dad if this gets deep and the cops come knocking on the door? All I needed was another fiasco. But this time around, it could be even more serious!

I figured my best plan of action was to wait until everything cooled down. I was trying to be optimistic. For the rest of the ride back home, all of these negative thoughts were going through my head. I tried to stay calm and not show any sign of panic. I didn't want Dom to know I was nervous.

When we finally got back to my house, I tried to keep myself calm while dividing up the cash for the day. I needed to put what had just happened behind me and bring my focus back to the present moment.

I picked up my money from the seat and put it in my pocket. I let Dom know I had a blast doing all of this but, I never wanted to do it again. He agreed and said it was great while it lasted, and I shouldn't worry too much about getting my ID taken away and that this would all work itself out.

I told Dom that I would figure out a way to get out from underneath all this because with all the crazy stuff I had done before, this would be just another walk in the park. He smiled, got back in his truck, and headed out; this would be the last time I would ever see him again.

I was out for good.

As I walked up to the front door, I was sweating bullets. I had so many mixed feelings. On one side I had made all this money and had the ride of my life! On the other hand, I had been caught by the bank and my ID and the bogus check were both confiscated. I could feel the insides of my body tighten up and my heart was pounding a mile a minute. I did not know what to say at this point because part of me believed everything was going to turn out all right and in the end, I shouldn't worry about it too much.

I also wanted to make sure I was not going to be taken down by this and have the rest of my life ruined. For just a moment, I was considering the idea of telling my dad what had just happened, but I quickly decided against it. Rolling the dice and staying quite was the best option, in my opinion.

Afterwards I went into my room to check on the proceeds of the last couple of days. Quietly I shut the door and sat down on my bed, taking all the cash out of my pockets and from my dresser drawer. My eyes lit up as I started to count all the money and separated the bills into different piles.

By the time I finished counting I could not contain my emotions! I had so much money in my hands! Sitting right in front of me was a pile of cash stacked up nice and high, but my thoughts went to how easy it had been.

When I snapped myself back to reality, I got up from my bed, picked up the stacks and put it all back in my top left dresser drawer. Out of nowhere a little light went off in my head. What if I did get caught and they wanted the money back? At this point, they did not know exactly how many checks I had cashed. As a precautionary measure, I took out two hundred dollars, walked across the bedroom, reached up to the top shelf on the wall and put the money as far back as I could.

Afterwards I felt a little more at ease because now I had my "out money" put away and would explain to the cops this was all the money I had made from cashing the checks. If anything were to happen, my basics would be taken care of.

Now comes the fun part-what would I buy with all this money? I wanted to spend as much of it as possible before I left for basic training!

Chapter Thirty-Three

Now I needed to have some type of transportation because, after all, I did not want to have to worry about relying on someone else to drive me around. More importantly, I needed something small so I could hide it from my parents. A car was not going to work since it would be difficult to hide. I decided to call up another friend of mine and see if he had any ideas about my transportation issue.

My friend had suggested I get a scooter, it was practical and would be the perfect solution. More so, I could easily hide it from my parents! I got excited because I knew I wanted one and had the cash to buy it outright!

Over the next few days, I did some calling around to see how close a dealership was to my house. After all, I still needed to get to a dealership and I couldn't ask my dad for a ride! After some searching, I narrowed it down to one specific dealership that could make this happen. I called up a friend of mine and he gave me a ride over.

Once we both got there, I talked to the owner for a little bit and he showed me around to what he had in stock. He had all kinds of models but I needed one that I could easily stash inside the garage to hide it as much as I could from my parents. I did some test driving and found the perfect little model! It could get me where I needed to go, but most importantly, small, and compact enough for me to cover up in the garage.

Now that I found the scooter I wanted, I gave the owner the thumbs up. He then gave me the numbers breakdown on what it will cost. Once we agreed on the price, he wrote up the bill of sale and I placed the cash down to take care of it.

As soon as he collected the cash and I collected the receipt, I was now officially able to take off anytime I wanted to! I was no longer dependent on a friend for a ride. Or for that matter, dependent on public transportation and all there crazy schedules!

Right after he gave me the keys, I started that bad boy up, twisting the throttle as hard as I possibly could! It made a small revving noise and didn't have much horsepower. In this particular case mule power because it only went 40 m.p.h. But in my mind, that revving sound was a sound of freedom and the ability to come and go whenever possible. It was going to work out perfectly!

Once I hoped onto the scooter, I circled around the parking lot for a few laps, just to get used to operating the scooter. After a few laps and getting to know how it operated, the owner gave me a helmet and thanked me for the business. I shook his hand, put the helmet on and I was off flying down the street cranking it up to a blustering 40 miles per hour!

As I was on the street heading back home, one thing had finally crossed my mind as I was driving the scooter. Holy shit! I didn't have a license! I just bought this scooter and had no idea what I was doing with it! I figured at this point, what was the worst that could happen? Kill myself for one, but I thought if I don't do anything stupid, I should be good! All I could do was laugh at that point because I did something stupid to get the cash to buy the scooter and was now also doing something even more stupid by driving it without a license!

When I got back home, I immediately went into the garage and parked the scooter. It fit perfectly between some stuff, which made it easy to hide. After all the excitement of buying the scooter, I wanted to go back out and spend some more money! I was now going out more and more, buying what I wanted, whenever I wanted! In that moment life was great. What was the possibility I would keep having fun without anything ever happening from the confiscated ID?

But just as life seemed to be at its highest moment, the opposite could also happen when it all fell apart.

I couldn't put my finger on it but that empty pit in the back of my gut kept saying, "It's only a matter of time before all of this came crashing down." Relatively soon for that matter!

It came about one day when I was at home, counting all my cash in the bedroom. I had heard the phone ring and didn't think anything of it. For all I knew, it was someone calling him for work. My dad went into the kitchen and picked up the phone.

When he picked up the phone, instantly I could tell something was wrong because there were long pauses between each of his sentences. More so, the tone of his voice went from pleasant to, dictator in the matter of a few sentences. Well, I could tell after those very short sentences, it wasn't his work calling him. But I think it was mostly from his specific words of, "What the hell did Eric do?" that truly put me in the moment of being called out on this!

Well, that person on the other end of the phone…was someone calling from the police department. Everything had finally caught up to me. The cat was officially let out of the bag.

"Oh shit!" I yelled out loud! I was frozen right where I was sitting, cash in my hand and on the bed from where I was counting it. My mind started to shift into overdrive with what I was going to do or say for that matter.

I looked down at the cash in my hands and threw it all down on the bed. All the while wiping my hands on my shirt as to get all of the dirtiness off. Once again my desire for excitement had caught to me and it was now time to pay the bill that was called due!

Scenario after scenario was dancing inside my head as I started to think up a story on how my ID had been stolen. "Was there anyway I could possibly come up with something that was going to save my bacon?" I thought to myself. I knew I needed something and fast!

After thinking everything through for a few minutes, one scenario in particular seemed to be the most believable.

My story was going to be that I went down to the beach a few weeks back with some friends and while we were on the waterfront, I had left my ID and some other things on the front seat of my friend's car. After being down in the water for a while, we all decided to leave and that's when we all noticed that his car had been broken into! Everything from inside the car had been taken, even is stereo system!

Once I discovered my ID had been stolen, I went down to the DMV shortly after and filled out the paperwork for a new one. Which was actually true since I had copies of the paperwork filled out for a new one.

"Yes!" I thought! This was my story and it was going to work! It was full proof!

I knew once my dad was off the phone, he was going to call me into the living room and ask me some questions. After about a fifteen-minute conversation with the police, like clockwork, my dad yelled out for me to join him in the living room. Just like I knew he would.

I walked out of the bedroom as calmly as I could because, after all, *I had not done anything wrong! It wasn't my fault someone had stolen my ID and used it for something as bad as cashing a fake check, right?* That was my story, and I was sticking to it!

I walked out into the living room and saw my dad standing with a pissed off look on his face. It was more the look that he always gave when he stared at you, as if he was piercing straight through your soul! You couldn't even look at him when he gave you that death stare because you literally felt like your entire body was going to melt down into a molten mound of fiery mass!

I knew I had to play it cool as soon as I sat down on the couch or I would surely give everything away on what I had done. And I sure as hell didn't want to tell him what I actually had done! He got right to the point and started to ask me all kinds of questions about my ID. Questions like, what day it happened, what time it happened, who was there that also saw the damage, etc. These were answers I knew I mentally had to take notes of just in case they came back up in the future.

I told him the scenario that I had played out in my head a few times, just so I had it down pat. I told him the exact story of a couple of weeks ago when it had been stolen from a friend's car while we were at the beach. Right after we got back, I went to the DMV and reported it stolen.

He then asked me "What was this about you trying to cash a fake corporate check?" I said, "It must have been someone else who was trying to cash a fake check with my stolen ID because it wasn't me."

After responding back to his question, I stared at him for a few seconds with a bewildering and puzzled look on my face as if to say, *what on earth are you talking about? It was not me who did it; it was the person who took my ID.*

I didn't say very much to him with each question as I was trying to be as vague as I could possibly be. I even went with the answering a question with a question bit for a little bit with, him asking, "Who's car was it who had been broken into?" and I said, "Who's car do you think it was who got broken into?" just to see how long I could hold out answering.

I tried to play it off and avoided all of his direct questions with as much fluff as I could possibly spew out of my mouth. After a few minutes of being bombarded with questions, he realized I wasn't going to say anything, since I was sticking by my story. I kept playing the, "It was a *someone else who did it*" and I was *"Totally innocent"* card.

I then asked him calmly, "Do you have any more questions for me?" and he said, "Yes but I'm going to let them go for the time being." I then breathed a sigh of relief and told him, 'I will be in my room if you can think of anything else." I got up from the couch and headed back into my room without saying another word.

I was thinking that if anything happened to me with this and I didn't get into the Navy, it would be the end of my life as I knew it! I told him everything was good and headed back to my room with a small smile on my face, as though this would all work itself out.

I figured this whole mess would just go away and it will work itself out…

Chapter Thirty-Four

What I didn't plan on was what my dad was going to do to me over the next couple of days. He was by no means going to drop this and would keep hammering away with questions, one after another. He was constantly asking all kinds of things like, "When was it stolen, were where you exactly when it happened?" I mean he was coming at me with everything! He was even writing down my answers on paper! I never thought he would take it this far, not in the slightest, but man, did he ever! He would blast me with questions anytime one popped up in his head.

Even when I went out for the day, he would ask me something before I left and the minute I stepped back into the house, he would continue firing off questions. It had finally come to the point where I was staying out all day to avoid being bombarded.

The questions continued for several days, until we got another phone call but this time it was from a different department, the Fraud Investigation Unit. Now this was getting serious! I had just come home and was headed to my room to put some things away when I heard my dad on the phone. I tried to listen in on the conversation, but it would be a very short one, since I heard my dad yell out really loudly, "What do you mean we have to come down to the station?"

My heart started to pound really loud and I could feel drops of sweat sliding down my face; this was, more like the *oh shit* kind of moment! As soon as my dad blurted out those words, he told them, “Fine, will be leaving shortly.”

I paused in the hallway to listen to what was going on and as soon as I heard my dad hang up the phone, I quietly walked back into my room and kept quiet. When I heard his footsteps coming out of the kitchen and towards my room, I put on my innocent look, waiting to see what he had to say. He walked in, looked at me and immediately said, “Get ready. We’re leaving for the police station!”

In my mind I had done absolutely nothing wrong, and this didn't faze me one bit because after all, I was innocent. You have to love the narcissism! I asked him what was going on and why we were going to the station. He gave me a crazed look and all he said was get ready because were leaving in a couple of minutes.

Quickly, we got ready, flew out the door and headed over to the office. For the entire drive over, not a word was said. The silence was nerve racking and so many thoughts were spinning through my head. Questions like, *what did they have on me? How many checks did they come up with that I had cashed*?

I tried to stay as calm as possible for the entire ride because I definitely did not want to look nervous or tip anything off which would make me look more guilty. I was constantly thinking that I might be caught for this!

As we pulled up to the station, my dad asked me point blank, "Is there anything I should know before we go inside?" I replied, "Not a thing, I don't know what they wanted to ask me."

I can remember him looking at me and just staring, probably wondering what was going through my head. He was looking to see if I was going to say anything and admit some type of wrongdoing. I kept rolling the dice to take my chances with all of this. He waited a couple of seconds for me to come clean and when nothing else was said, we walked out of the car and headed into the office.

We walked up to the front counter and notified the clerk we were here for some questioning. She escorted us back into one of the rooms where an agent was waiting for me. The agent opened the door and told me to come in. My dad was right behind me, but the agent told him I was here for some questioning, and he should have a seat outside until were finished. When he closed the door, I noticed the walls were glass and when you sat outside the office you would be looking directly back into the room.

I sat down in the chair and looked over my shoulder to see my dad sitting on a bench, wearing sunglasses, and staring right at me through the windows. I didn't know what made me more nervous, an agent asking me questions, or my dad staring right through my soul!

After we were seated, I was a nervous wreck. I could not focus as my mind was wandering all over the place. I kept telling myself I was innocent and there was absolutely nothing wrong. The agent didn't say anything at first and all he did was grab his files on the desk. He opened them up and finally spoke.

His first words were "You're not under arrest. Your here because you tried to cash a fake corporate check and got caught." I looked at the officer and replied, "Fake check? What on earth are you talking about? I never tried to cash any type of check. Where would I even get something like that?"

He just stared back at me and replied, "Let's stop with the bullshit. You were caught inside a bank trying to cash a check which was fake, and you were identified by the teller in a photo lineup." I tried to say everything and anything I could to get out of the situation but when I finally came to grips, I realized that all I was doing was pissing this guy off, so I tried to think of a way to smooth this over.

I started to poke around and ask him some questions. I asked him how they identified me from the get-go? He reached into the file and pulled out about four pages of photos with each having four squares with a picture of a different persons face on them. Then he told me the teller had identified my face through a picture line up which was how she was able to finger me for the check.

Damn! I felt myself going into panic mode and hitting the, "Oh Shit!" button because I was now being challenged by the agent! I felt my wheels starting to spin and took a couple of seconds to think before I started to answer his questions. I tilted my head down and started to think of the saddest thought I could put in my mind. I made myself cry a little to bring on the sadness. When I got myself looking all pathetic and sad, I looked back up at the officer and the next question he asked was, "How did you do it?"

I asked for clarification and said, "How did I get the checks or how did I get to the banks and cash them?" He replied, "How did you get mixed up in this and how did you get the checks."

I was not going to tell him the true story because there was no way I was going to be "ratting" anyone out. If I ever got into trouble and it was me and only me, I was going to take the blame for whatever happened and do everything I could to get out of it.

Now that my thoughts were back into focus, my mind went into a total creative mode. I started to tell him what happened while creating a story in mere seconds as he wanted me to describe every moment of how it all unfolded. I now had the perfect plan down! Starting with the tears running down my face, I was ready to talk so I began to spin off a made-up scenario…

It all began at the Buena Park mall when a guy approached me and asked if I wanted to make some quick cash. I told him I was not interested but the more I said no, the more persistent he became.

Quickly the agent wrote everything down and I continued by saying that as I started to walk away from the guy, he kept following me around and wasn't going to stop following me until I did what he asked. Finally, I gave in and asked the guy what the plan was. He said all we were going to do was go into a bank and cash some checks and afterwards, he would pay me with no questions asked.

I had to make the story as convincing as possible so when the agent asked me to describe what the guy looked like, I made up someone who was about six feet four inches tall and weighed about two hundred pounds. He was skinny and wore baggy clothes to make it look like he was hiding something in his clothes.

I could not believe my own ears! I was spitting this stuff out so fast! It was crazy how I was making up some guy out of nowhere! I went on for a few minutes describing this fictional character and when I finished up with my description, I told the agent the guy was very overbearing, and they should watch out for him because of the way he portrayed himself.

He was taking everything in and then shifted gears and asked how many checks he had given me to cash? All I could say was only four before I got caught. Still having the tears in my eyes and keeping my head down, he asked me how much money I made from the checks.

Ah yes, the money I had stashed on the top shelf in my bedroom. Only about two hundred dollars which was all I got for him.

Still writing everything down, he turned to me and asked if there was anything else I could think of which would help my case? Everything I could think of was out in the open and I told the agent, "I hope they catch the guy who created this mess, and I am deeply sorry for my actions."

He finished writing up his statements and said I was free to go because I was only a small fish in the pond; they wanted the top dog of the food chain.

My sadness and tears stopped as quickly as they started, and I asked if I was free to go? "Yes", he said, "But stick around because we may have more questions sometime in the future."

Just for safety's sake I poured on a little more of a pity card, letting him know I was leaving for basic training at the end of the year. If he had anything else for me, I would be around until I shipped out. He got up from his chair, opened the door and I walked out with a sense of awe. I had just put on the academy award performance of my life, getting myself out of this catastrophe! What a wake-up call this was!

From that point on I was officially done with being stupid. I didn't want anything to screw me up from entering the Navy. I was one hundred percent serious this time! I was truly finished with getting myself into trouble and I needed a fresh start in the Navy.

I walked out of the office with the agent as he told my dad there wasn't anything serious in the matter. My dad looked at the agent and said a few words but didn't listen. I had too many other thoughts spinning through my head.

He gave us his card and while we were walking out the agent mentioned, if I heard anything else from the guy at the mall, I needed to call him right away. All I could think of at this point was, Holy crap! I just escaped from something major!

As we headed out to the car, my dad asked me what that was all about and I told him it was all a misunderstanding. I was not the person they were looking for, which was partially true! He looked at me, shook his head, and as usual didn't say anything more. What more was there to say? I wasn't arrested for any crime, and no one was pressing any charges.

I could tell he had his doubts because after all, who goes into the special crimes office for questioning and comes out without any type of damage?

As usual it was another quiet ride back home and all I did was look out the window and think about the "what if's" and boy were there some crazy "what ifs!" At this point, I could throw the "what if's" out the window, because I could not concern myself with the negative possibilities.

Chapter Thirty-Five

I knew I had to tell my recruiter what happened, so as soon as went inside the house, I told my dad I needed to go over to the recruiter's office and give him an update on what had just happened. I quickly went into my room, grabbed my keys, and headed out to the garage. I took my BMX bike as I didn't want to arouse suspicion with my scooter. I wanted to keep that as quiet as possible, for as long as I could.

When I arrived at the recruiter's office, he was busy with another person and I was asked to take a seat. After he was finished, he called me over and I sat down at his desk. He asked, "What's going on and you do you look so frazzled?" Quickly I blurted out the entire story. I mean I gave up every single detail! Every real detail! I began with how it all started, how many checks

I cashed and the end result in just getting back from the fraud investigation office!

My recruiter looked at me in total disbelief. He turned to me and said, "You're messing with me, aren't you? It's all a joke, right?"

"Stay out of trouble." Was his words that I needed to take more seriously!

I looked at him square in the face and said, "I literally just got back from the fraud investigation office after being questioned on what I had done!" To top it off, I pulled out the agent's card and showed it to him. I said, "Here's the proof and the name of the agent I was speaking too." He now knew I was not playing around and that I was serious about what was going on.

Seeing his facial expression, I needed to get a gauge of what he was thinking. He was stuck looking at the card I gave him, trying to get an idea of what to say. I waited for a few seconds so he could soak it all in, but I could tell by his dazed look he was going to need more time.

As he started to come around and get his focus back, he said, "Hang tight Eric because I need to figure something out really quickly." He went over to his desk and I took a seat in one of the chairs. In my mind, the clock was ticking, in that f the fraud investigator wanted to push the issue and press charges, I needed to be out of California and in Basic Training sooner rather than later.

I sat waiting patiently at his desk as he made a couple of phone calls. One by one he sped through each call trying to get the best case scenario he could get. I heard things like, "Correct, fraud investigation talked to him," "Yes it was confirmed he did it," and "We need to move quickly."

At this point, it seemed as if time had stood still because all I could do was keep looking at the clock as every second passed by and wait for an answer.

Finally, after what had felt like an eternity, he hung up the phone and looked at me squarely in the eyes and said, "I found you a solution to this problem." "Great!" I shouted and I gave a deep sigh of relief! "Not so fast." He said right after I let out all of my air. He went on to say, "Since we now have to work around this problem, I am now going to be moving up your basic training ahead of schedule."

I asked him, "What does that mean moving my training ahead of schedule?" My original date was set for December but now he needed to make some changes and move me up a couple of months sooner. Instead of leaving when I was supposed to, I was now leaving at the end of October!

He said, "This was the best I could do and now you need to get ready to leave and quickly!" This meant it gave me 2 less months to get everything ready before I left. He asked, "Are you willing and able to get through this process a lot sooner?" I replied, "No problem and I am willing to do whatever it takes to get this all being me." "Good, I'm glad to hear it and I will be in touch with your new paperwork."

I got up from his desk and said, "Thanks for understanding and doing what you just did to make this all happen."

As I headed to the door, I was still a bit frazzled with what all that just happened. Especially with putting myself in this position to begin with! Now I needed to get back and tell my parents that my time frame had been moved up and I needed to fly out 2 months sooner than planned.

Just as I was about to jump on my bike and head back home, he quickly walked out of the office and shouted to me saying, **"Eric, For the love of God stay out of trouble until you leave for bootcamp!"** I looked at him and said, "I'm going to be living under a rock for the next couple of months, until I'm ready to leave with plane tickets in my hand!"

He started to laugh as I turned away to peddle back home.

When I got home, I told my dad my leave date was pushed up by a couple of months, because of this fiasco. All he said was, "Good, the sooner you left the better!" I stood there for a second and laughed because for once I totally agreed with him! When it was all said and done, I went into my room and chilled out for the rest of the day thinking about all the events from the past few weeks.

It had been a real crazy ride and one that I will never forget, but one ride I was soon hoping to put behind me for good.

Chapter Thirty-Six

I found myself caring less and less about the job I was doing at Knott's because it got old really fast. Technically I was supposed to be working there until I left for the Navy, but after about two months on the job, I got fired for playing around too much and not taking the job seriously. It was fine with me because I was already mentally checked out anyway.

It was also during this time my dad found out I had a scooter and, of course, it did not go over very well. To him I was always full of surprises, and mostly not the most pleasant kind. So today would be no exception. It was early in the day and when I got back home, I parked my scooter in the garage and walked into the house. My dad looked at me and asked why I was home so early, I told him flat out that I just got fired and was done working.

"Fired! What the Hell do you mean you just got fired!" I told him I didn't care about the job; I really wasn't taking it seriously. I still had a lot of money left over so I was not too worried.

He asked me the all-important question: *How I got back home so quickly*. That I did not have an answer for. I stumbled for words, desperately trying to think of something believable. I had nothing, so, I decided to come clean. I told him I bought a scooter several weeks ago. Of course, he wanted to know where I got the money.

That question, of course, I did not answer. I deflected by saying the scooter was out in the garage and if he wanted to go look, its sitting right as you open the door. He really thought I was playing around and decided to call my bluff.

As he got up from the couch, he grabbed the garage keys and went out to look. What could he really say since I bought it with my own money? When he returned, he was shaking his head back and forth in disbelief.

He sat back down on the couch still shaking his head. I asked him if there was anything else he wanted to talk about, but he didn't say a word.

I walked back into the room and hung out for the rest of the day listening to my music.

The months turned into weeks and the weeks turned into days so I knew it was only a matter of time before I was saying my goodbyes to everyone. I felt like I needed to spend as much time with everyone as I could because, once I left, life was going to change, not only for me but for everyone else as well.

The days finally ticked down to house and before I knew it, the day had come for me to get my bag ready and head out the door.

Around 5:30 a.m. I got up and got ready for the long day that was ahead of me. I got my bag together and took a seat on the couch waiting for the van to come by and pick me up. I said to myself, "You did it!" "You made it all the way to this point and now you were about to move ahead with life!" I was nervous, anxious, but most of all, excited about this opportunity. This was something I was going to give everything I got, both physically and mentally until I completed every step of Boot Camp.

Just as I was about to get up from the couch, I heard a honk at the end of the driveway. I looked out the window and there was a van waiting outside ready to take me to the airport. I gave everyone hugs, grabbed what little I had, jumped in the van, and closed the door.

This was the life changing moment I had been waiting for! It had finally arrived and I was going to make the most of it! It had felt like an eternity, but as the van drove off, I looked back and knew from this point on, my life was going to change forever. I was really excited for a fresh start.

In what seemed like the longest ride ever, we got to the airport and headed over to our terminal. We had to sit around for a little while waiting to board our plane. It was the usual hurry up and wait bit with any airport. Finally, our flight was called over the intercom and our group boarded the plane and we all took our seats. I got my bag all stowed away and took my seat.

I was all belted in and waiting for take-off while my heart was pounding a mile a minute. I heard the jet engines fire up and the stewards gave us the preflight information and were now cleared for take-off! I leaned back in my seat and as the plane took off from the ground, I smiled and waved goodbye to my troubled past. I was now putting it all behind me and moving forward.

Once we were airborne, I knew there was no turning back. I was super excited to get to basic training! All I could do was keep staring out the window as each state flew by, as if each one represented a part of my past floating away.

After we landed and got off the plane, I realized that it was winter in Illinois: it was fricking freezing! How's that for a new beginning. I was not in California anymore.

We took a van over to the processing unit where we needed to check in before we got shifted over to our new homes. It was almost nerve wracking at first because I was so used to living my life a certain way. Mostly with no one telling me what I needed to do on a daily basis. We were about to be reprogrammed and molded in a way suited for a military life. This was going to be a big challenge for me. I was never a person who could be molded in certain ways. I hated following the norm and being a sheep. I had always done everything on my own. Micromanaging and I went together like oil and vinegar; it never came out on a positive outcome.

After getting ourselves checked in and settled into our barracks, we came in with literally only our clothes on our backs. I got my first look of military life when we were getting our new uniforms and had to change out of our street clothes. We had to send everything back home. Once we changed into our new uniforms and packed up our boxes, it seemed like I was becoming a new person, changing into a new way of life while shipping our old ways back home.

When one of the company commanders, in essence a drill instructor, was yelling at us, giving everyone instructions on what we needed to do, I asked him what we had to do with our electronic devices. Back then pagers were all the rage and cell phones were slowly working their way into mainstream society. When I asked him where I should put the pager, he literally looked at me and said, "You need to shut the F up and listen to what I am telling you!"

All I could do was just stand and grin because I did not know how to react to his comment. I took off the pager and took out the battery while dropping it in my ship out box. I was still grinning because of his response but I quickly dropped it and went about my business. I thought, welcome to the military!

Time seemed to be flying by because of how busy we were. We were either eating, exercising, putting on new uniforms, or learning all the new ways of military life. It was a whole new experience. Everyone was learning a lot and those who could not keep up with the program were left behind. Some of the people you started to get to know were gone within a couple of weeks because they failed their exams and got pushed back or got discharged for doing something prior to getting into bootcamp.

This was where I had to keep everything quiet with the corporate checks. My recruiter had warned me to keep my mouth shut. My thoughts were that if I made it through basic training, I would be part of the government and could not be touched by law enforcement. I was never arrested or convicted and I wanted to keep pushing forward.

Every day was the same: being on top of your game and learning everything you could, while keeping up with your physical exercises. One of the favorite training courses for most of the recruits was what they called the gas chamber. It was where you would go into a room wearing a gas mask and they would pop a canister of tear gas. Once the canister was in and smoking, they closed the doors and let the gas settle inside the room for a few minutes. You were then required to take off the mask and sing the Navy anthem all the while you were inhaling the gas into your lungs. When you were singing the gas would fill your body up and when your body tried to expel it, it all came out in different ways which looked really disgusting! People were starting to choke, hack their lungs up and fluids would come out from all over your face, choking on your own fluids and you would be trying to spit it all up.

Overall, it was a nasty sight to see and something I really did not want to do. I wanted to bypass this part of the basic training, skipping it all together. My wheels were starting to turn. *How was I going to get my ticket out of this*?

Right before our company was supposed to step in and enjoy the fresh new experience, we had to get cleared by our corpsman. He would authorize us to step inside and have an experience most of them were looking forward to.

As each one of us went through to get cleared, my wheels were turning and I was thinking of a way to get out of it. I was not sick or did not have any medical issues which would prevent me from participating in the fun.

I watched others in front of me also trying to get out of the chamber and our corpsman was not buying any of it. The other recruits were all coming out of line with a disappointed look on their face. My turn was next and when I walked inside to get checked out by the corpsman, I had to put on the academy award show.

It was Show Time as I pulled out all stops!

Standing right in front of me was my ticket to either doing the gas chamber or walking away from it. She started to ask me some medical questions on internal issues. Now was when I popped the question about the gas chamber. I asked if there was any way I could get out of not doing the gas chamber.

I told her I would keep my mouth shut and not say a word to anyone. I just played it off as all of the crazy stuff I had done before. I mean what was the worst that could happen? We chatted for a few minutes and she finally looked over at me and said, "If I give you a pass from the chamber, do you promise not to say a word?"

I looked back at her and said, "I promise I will not say a word to anyone and will keep it between us." She picked up my file and signed off that I was not cleared to do the gas chamber. I had talked my way out of the gas chamber and would be standing on the sideline! I had actually done it!

She folded my file, gave it back to me and when I hopped off the table gave me a water jog to hold onto as if to say I was sick and could not participate in the fun times. I took the jug and thanked her one more time before I left the examination room and headed back to my command. When I got back in line with the others and they saw me holding the water jug, they started to say I was scared, along with some other crap, but I didn't care.

I told them to have fun while getting gassed and that I would be watching every second of them looking like fools while I was laughing on the sidelines. It was a great feeling seeing all of them pissed, especially those who tried and failed on getting out of it.

When it came time for everyone to get into the chamber, I was on top of the world holding my water jug and watching everyone who came out of the room hacking their lungs out. Some of them even started to throw up inside their gas mask! It was getting way to nasty to watch. I was laughing my butt off especially at the ones with the smart-ass comments; it was awesome because I was taking a drink as they were all getting gassed up.

Finally, when the chamber ended, everyone was in a crazed state of mind from the gas and their fluids where everywhere. We all filed in and headed back to our barracks so everyone who was a mess could get changed. Right after, went to dinner and we continued on with our training for the day. It was straight back to business as usual with our command.

Our graduation was quickly approaching and we were still losing people in our command. Some were getting discharged by not disclosing personal information, like having criminal records. All I could do was keep looking forward and not say a word about anything from my past.

The sooner I could complete basic training, the quicker I could put my past behind me. Every day that passed by without me being called out for what I had done in my past, was another day closer to graduation.

Before we all knew it, graduation was finally here! Two and a half months had flown by in the blink of an eye and we were finally finished! I had made it.

Our day had finally come. We now joined the ranks of the armed forces, and I was officially part of the U.S. Navy! It was an awesome feeling! I felt like I was now part of something meaningful and it gave me a sense of accomplishment. I now belong to an organization which will always be looking out for me! If it all worked out, I might even want to stay in for the full twenty years and make it a career.

For the mean time I felt like I could accomplish anything!

After graduation, we said our goodbyes to each other and exchanged information with those we would keep in touch with. While we were checking out and getting our boarding passes back home, we were getting our orders and processing out of basic training.

We got our bags and headed to our designated vans waiting to take us back to the airport, knowing that I most likely would never see any of the others from basic training again. Overall, it was a great experience, full of ups and downs and emotions which will push you to your limits, one I would do all over again with no questions asked.

When we got to the airport, we were all wearing our new uniforms fresh from basic training! While I was waiting to board my flight, I was sitting constantly looking at my uniform. It was such a different feeling since I never imagined myself sitting halfway across the U.S. wearing a dress uniform. Never in my entire life could I have imagined this would happen.

I had made it through basic training without any issues! My past did not catch up to me and I was officially cleared! At one point I really thought I was dreaming. It never felt so real because of everything I had put myself through, I never thought I would make it out of basic training. Two and a half months flew by in the blink of an eye and I made it through!

Honestly, I thought the check issue would catch up to me and I would be one of the causalities who were dishonorably discharged for not disclosing my information. Luckily, I had a recruiter who pushed my leave date up and got me out of California as quickly as possible before something serious came up.

Now, I belonged to the U.S. Navy! Anything that would happen to me would now have to go through them, meaning if I had any troubles from my past the Navy would be there to take care of any issues.

The Navy would be looking out for me…

After graduation, we all got our assignments. Some were going to head off to their respective training schools. Others straight out to the fleet. I had to wait an extra two weeks before I headed back home since my training school was not quite ready.

Once the day came for me to pack up and leave, I grabbed all my bags, headed to the airport, and headed back home. I sat thinking the entire way back on the flight thinking about my next phase in life once I got back home. I was now ready to take on any challenge that was thrown my way.

A total of three months had passed by since I step foot in Great Lakes, when I arrived back in California. I got home and noticed that not only did my life change but most of my friends had also changed as well.

Life would never be the same again because I would now be traveling the world and going out to sea whenever possible. I got together with whomever was available, but most of them had moved on with their lives to and would now only see them every so often; we were all moving on with our next chapters in life, some of us for the better and some for the worse.

After learning the basics of Navy life and assimilating to the new lifestyle, I was now on my next phase. I would be checking into "A" school which was my job school and over the next four months, learning everything I could about what my job as a Navy cook.

The Navy truly gave me every opportunity to succeed. In fact, it was the best decision I had ever made in my life up to that moment in time. I was on the road to success and I could feel my personality changing for the better. No longer was I going to submit to my cravings and impulses, just for a few seconds of heavenly bliss.

The days of doing whatever I felt like doing and not thinking about my consequences were gone. Now, every action had a consequence and if it went wrong, I would be held accountable for those actions. I felt the Navy would give me that daily sense of excitement, but in a more constructive way. Now that I have a sense of purpose, I no longer needed to get my daily dose of adrenaline.

I finally reached the light at the end of the tunnel and it was the brightest light I had ever seen.

The future was mine to control and I was looking forward to every minute of it!

Bootcamp Completion 1994

References

*"The Signs and Symptoms of Adrenaline Addiction," *Mental health* (22, August 29), Web, Ashwood Recovery.

Adrenaline addict (ashwoodrecovery.com)

*"3 Signs That Your Adrenaline Addiction Is Wreaking Havoc," *Mental health* (23, January 13), Web, Ashwood Recovery.

Is It Possible Be Addicted to an Adrenaline Rush? (ashwoodrecovery.com)

Acknowledgements

I would like to give a big thanks to Jia Hamud, for taking all of my many revisions and putting them together!

Tina Gurney for story editing and making sense of what I was writing.

Drew Martinez for my book cover.

King Features Syndicate / North America Permissions A UNIT OF THE HEARST CORPORATION for allowing me to add a bit of humor in adding one of their cartoons to my book.

Thank you to all!

Made in the USA
Las Vegas, NV
05 April 2024

88304664R00144